1001

OUTDOOR SWIMMING TIPS

1001

OUTDOOR SWIMMING TIPS

ENVIRONMENTAL, SAFETY, TRAINING AND GEAR ADVICE FOR COLD-WATER, OPEN-WATER AND WILD SWIMMERS

calum maclean

Vertebrate Publishing, Sheffield
www.adventurebooks.com

1001

OUTDOOR
SWIMMING
TIPS

**ENVIRONMENTAL, SAFETY,
TRAINING AND GEAR ADVICE
FOR COLD-WATER, OPEN-WATER
AND WILD SWIMMERS**

calum maclean

First published in 2022 by Vertebrate Publishing.

Vertebrate Publishing
Omega Court, 352 Cemetery Road, Sheffield S11 8FT, United Kingdom.
www.adventurebooks.com

Copyright © 2022 Calum Maclean and Vertebrate Publishing.

Calum Maclean has asserted his rights under the Copyright,
Designs and Patents Act 1988 to be identified as author of this work.

A CIP catalogue record for this book is available from the British Library.

ISBN 978-1-83981-123-4 (Paperback)
ISBN 978-1-83981-124-1 (Ebook)

Front cover illustration © Julia Allum represented by www.meiklejohn.co.uk
Photography by Calum Maclean unless otherwise credited.

Edited by Jess McElhattan, design by Nathan Ryder, production by Terry Yeardley,
C2 Clear Creative.

Printed and bound in Europe by Latitude Press.

Vertebrate Publishing is committed to printing on paper from sustainable sources.

Every effort has been made to achieve accuracy of the information in
this guidebook. The authors, publishers and copyright owners can take
no responsibility for: loss or injury (including fatal) to persons; loss or
damage to property or equipment; trespass, irresponsible behaviour
or any other mishap that may be suffered as a result of following the
advice offered in this guidebook.

SAFETY STATEMENT

Outdoor and wild swimming are activities that carry a risk of personal injury or death. Participants
must be aware of and accept that these risks are present and they should be responsible for
their own actions and involvement. Nobody involved in the writing and production of this
guidebook accepts any responsibility for any errors that it may contain, nor are they liable for
any injuries or damage that may arise from its use. Outdoor swimming and particularly wild
swimming are inherently dangerous and the fact that individual descriptions in this volume do
not point out such dangers does not mean that they do not exist. Take care.

contents

introduction

'You never regret a swim.'

This is a philosophy to try and live by when it comes to swimming outdoors. I say *try* to live by, as when there's an icy wind, grey skies and dark water in the thick of winter, it can be very easy to ask, *why am I doing this?* The big 'WHY?' is a question that gets asked by family, friends, puzzled onlookers and even curious animals. At times, the truth of 'why' does not come during the swim, but in the aftermath: in shared tales of water with friends; in the look across the sea to a distant island; in the glow of heat returning to once-frozen toes; in the realisation of, *wow, I just did that*; in the sheer buzz that zips around your body after leaving the water and comes flying out of your mouth in a howl.

At times, it can feel like type II fun. Having said that, it doesn't need to be a struggle. We can find the joy and truth within the activity: the feeling of gliding through calm water, the zen-like state reached after hours of left, right, breathe, left, right, breathe, the power of controlling our breath and getting over that initial shock upon entry. There's also the learning of new and exotic ways to swear and entertain the wise, towel-holding friends.

I've loved the water since I was a child. Many of my family holidays involved camping trips and in my memory I was constantly in or around water. I didn't grow up as a competitive swimmer, and it wasn't until my very late teens and early twenties that I became hooked and eventually addicted. I got into triathlons and trail running, and I'd often try and combine this with a swim. I was still not competitive or very fast in races, and eventually realised that competitive-ness against others doesn't motivate me: much of my love of outdoor swimming comes from finding new experiences and locations. I can get bored of swimming in one place, so to spend hours seeking a dunk in a far-off river pool is, for me, an ideal way to spend a day.

A number of years ago, miserable in my work, I'd spend almost all my free time going out finding new places to swim. The freedom and buzz I'd get from 'discovering' a new, hidden waterfall or bay that I'd yet to swim in made me feel alive. From this, I started to document swims, firstly through photos and writing a blog and then videos on the BBC The Social platform. This opened up the opportunity to film three series of *Dhan Uisge (Into the Water)* on BBC ALBA, my outdoor swimming series where I'd take on the most interesting or unusual swims I could think up. The BBC always wanted them to be filmed in winter for some reason …

The majority of my swimming has been in Scotland, as it's where I live and where I feel I'm meant to be. In Scotland we have such a variety of swimming opportunities, from the frozen ice in winter and kilometres and kilometres of lochs for endurance swimming to crystal-clear pools (if you know where to look). We even have the very occasional warm-water days in a hot summer – well, we have small warm patches, within some lochs. And usually only at the surface …

All swimmers enjoy it for their own reasons: some want the challenge and focus of long-distance swims, others just enjoy being in the cold. This book looks at all the types and aspects of swimming, with a focus on what I know.

I am an average swimmer – maybe I'm not even average. I've not swum across the Channel, and a decent 14-year-old swimmer in training could smoke me in a race … maybe even a 12-year-old, I don't know how fast they swim. But I have done, and do, swim a lot. I've made very silly mistakes, I've taken part in races, I've swum down sketchy rivers and under

Jumping for joy in Montenegro.

ice and pushed myself into being an all-year-round swimmer. I wear a wetsuit, and I wear nothing at all. I've tried to swim every day for a year three times, and failed each time. Through failure and success, I've learnt a lot. As I get older I feel my focus turn more towards the endurance aspects – this might just come with age – but I'll never lose the joy of leaping into a waterfall pool.

I love to inspire and encourage others to swim, or simply to try the water, so they can find out for themselves what they love about it. As much as swimming outdoors grows as a 'thing', what could be a hindrance to some people taking part is the activity becoming framed by one particular view; as though it can only be seen through one lens, or as if it should only be enjoyed in one way. The 'WHY?' question that attracts many people also raises many a derisive or skeptical eyebrow. The sport of open-water swimming and swimming outdoors as a hobby is not new, despite a recent surge in people taking to the water. I know record-setting marathon swimmers, ice-milers (*tips 443–446*) and dippers who only do it for their mental health – often they'll all swim together.

Within this book I hope to give tips and information that could help all swimmers, no matter their experience or interest. It's a compilation of things I have learnt, and much of this has come through experience, and failure at times. I've learnt these tips by meeting and listening to other swimmers, and from viewing how people take on swims. Some knowledge has come from sitting and staring at the surface water of a river pool from below. Maybe all the tips will be useful for you; maybe none at all. Maybe I'll look back at the book in 20 years and have 500 tips I'd throw away and 500 new ones. But one tip will always remain: there's enough space in the water for everyone.

This book is not and can't be a replacement for going out and swimming safely with people; from being open to trying new experiences and pushing yourself. You'll notice the tone shifts radically, often within the same paragraph or sentence: dark humour sits alongside inspirational guff. It might not go directly from A to B, but instead include diversions to F, Q and R along the way. It's probably a fair representation of my brain. A bit like that time I set out to swim and walk from coast to coast across Scotland – I did it, but via some hitch-hiking to the doctor en route, and a swim inside a tunnel … but that's a story best told in person.

This book and the information within it should be useful and make you smile. Or smirk. It's got some nice pictures and places for you to swim anyway.

acknowledgements

Firstly, I'd like to thank my parents, Kerrie and Ruairidh, for their constant support and for giving me a love of the outdoors, adventure and swimming from an early age, and my partner Hannah, who has helped dress my cold body on many a windy shoreline.

I'd like to thank Kate Rew and the entire Outdoor Swimming Society, who helped grow my love for swimming, Vivienne Rickman and Alan Corcoran, who contributed to locations for the book, and Muslim Alim, who opened one door that led to so many opportunities.

To Sara Barnes, Suzanna Cruickshank and Rachel Whitfield, who all contributed to sections to this book, I am hugely grateful.

Thank you to Kirsty Reade and all at Vertebrate Publishing for giving me this opportunity, and Jessica McElhattan, who helped guide and shape my thoughts into a coherent, actual book.

Lastly, thank you to the outdoor swimming community, a supportive, vibrant and diverse collection of people – I'm grateful to be a part of this world.

feedback and updates

If you have any feedback or questions about this book, or updates to information within the book, I can be contacted at *calumswims@gmail.com*

My website is **caldamac.com**

I can be followed on social media *@caldamac*

Warning: this photo may contain bare feet.

A stunning swim in Glencoe, Scotland.

There's no such thing as a bad place to brush up on your Gaelic.

001

BASICS (1–194)

'Faigh cuidhteas air an ràmh, dhan a' chladach,
nì mi shnàmh.
"Get rid of the oar, I'll swim to shore."
Not at all an ancient Scottish Gaelic proverb'

Look out, there's an orca behind you!

BASICS (1–194)

25 REASONS WHY (OR WHAT TO TELL PEOPLE WHO JUST DON'T 'GET IT') (1–25)

1. So that you can tell everyone you meet that you swim outdoors. It's a kind of shibboleth: once you tell someone that you're into it, if they respond with enthusiasm then you're probably going to get along. If they look at you with suspicion, just remember they don't yet know what they're missing out on.

2. Turn your frown upside down. It will put a spring in your step all day. Even that mental boost of getting into the water initially can change how you feel and give you a super-charged positive attitude. It's that moment of clarity as you overcome fear and expel doubt from your mind. It can be a way of rediscovering your child-like, fun side. Any swim, no matter how small, can feel like an adventure. I find an early morning swim is particularly useful ahead of a busy or potentially stressful day – getting an early win under your belt is good for the soul.

3. So you that can start a blog, telling everyone that comes across it that you swim outdoors. Good luck finding a new and unused variation of the words 'wild' and 'swim' for your title, though; I had a swimming blog (long since unused), *goneoffswimming.wordpress.com* – a future-proofed title if I get sick of swimming one day!

4. To learn some cool new party tricks. Ever seen a finger turn almost transparent, or been able to kick a door with your bare feet and not feel any pain at all? Well, who wants to be able to feel their toes anyway? This was the case for me for around a month due to a very poorly planned journey to and from a cold swim. I'm not saying I recommend it, but it was a good lesson learnt: wear footwear that keeps your feet warm and dry.

5. So you can tweet about the joys of outdoor swimming. Who knows, this might even lead to an article for *The Guardian*.

6. It's an excuse to eat cake. I think this might actually be the key motivator for many swimmers: the post-swim cake. While this can unite the community, it can also cause hours of debate. What's my favourite? For me, it is a nod to my Australian roots with lamingtons – read on for the recipe (*tip 298*).

7. The community and friends you'll make. Outdoor swimming gives you a feeling of belonging; you'll become part of a tribe, pod, club or group. This might at first be an online group, where you initially watch from a distance before dipping a toe in, before meeting actual, real-life swimmers. It's a huge and growing community. You will meet inspiring people and swimmers who will help you not only learn about your limits, but overcome them.

8. This is often the best way to gain knowledge, confidence, experience and cakes. The bonus of being in a group is that by just baking one cake, you might actually get to eat six or seven other ones too.

9. For the swears you'll learn. You might rate yourself as having a pretty crude turns of phrase, but wait until you hear variations of curses added together to create whole new meanings. I love regional variants – any new group of swimmers will have their own language system to describe the cold, and usually with plenty of swears as part of it.

10. So you can proudly post in a Facebook group about the joys of winter swimming. Maybe *The Independent* will pick this up.

11. The glamour and smugness as you get changed awkwardly in a cold, wet, windy car park, spilling coffee all over yourself from uncontrollably shaking hands. It's the perfect excuse to buy that changing robe.

12. To travel and see the most incredible places. It's not all about being cold and huddling under a giant robe: once you start to consider swimming as a reason to travel, a whole new world opens up. From Arabian wadis to the azure-coloured seas of Belize and the seemingly endless lakes of Italy, the world is full of stunning locations, challenging swims and historic venues.

13. To transform how you look at any body of water. Outdoor swimming will help break up long, boring car journeys with new dunks; any trip is transformed when you view it through your swimmer's eyes. A dull section of motorway might hide a secret river pool, right underneath your tyres; an out-of-view section of coastline could be that next special beach.

14. To get you through winter. Having a focus and embracing the seasons can really help you to feel that they go by quicker. At the very least it's an excuse to wear 10 fleeces in winter all at once.

15. So you can write a blog post about how you've always just called it 'swimming', without any prefix. *The Telegraph* will soon come knocking.

16. The pain relief of water. Cold-water swimming recovery has long been used by athletes to allow their muscles to recover after exercise, but using cold water to relieve chronic pain is growing in popularity. Just being in water also removes the weight and pressure from joints, making it an ideal activity for all ages.

17. Swimming is a vital life skill. Many people would panic if they suddenly dropped into water and were forced to swim any distance, yet swimming in open water is a skill that the vast majority are capable of, if they choose to learn it. There may come a day when you are forced into swimming, so why not get that capacity and skill mastered on your own terms?

18. To tap into something primal. There's something deep inside us, a connection to the water, that you may not even realise exists until you take the plunge and swim. It can become addictive. There is something to suggest that outdoor swimming is actually 'the truth' – it just makes sense to do, and needs no clear explanation.

19. To escape flies, insects and beasties: they often won't travel far from the shore, so taking yourself off into deep water is the perfect antidote to getting devoured by mosquitoes or midgies on a summer evening.

20. So you can declare in an online article that there are just too many people nowadays swimming outdoors. *The Daily Mail* might enjoy that.

21. There are no lanes, black lines or tumble turns. Okay, there may be at lidos (which are also great), but having the power and responsibility to decide how to swim and look after yourself is freeing. You're forced to think for yourself, make mistakes, learn from them and then make the right decisions. It's akin to the difference between running on a treadmill or pounding the pavement and then running on trails or mountains: I occasionally do one, so that I can really enjoy and thrive at the other.

22. Just so that passing walkers can shout, 'You must be maaad!' at you. I've yet to actually convert a bewildered onlooker in the moment, but the more we swim and encourage others to do so, the more we normalise it. Otherwise, it may become frowned upon, viewed with suspicion or even prohibited in some places.

23. Yeah, staring at swimming pool tiles for hours is nice enough, but have you ever had a gaggle of honking geese soar above you on a silent, misty morning? Have you floated above a parrotfish, nibbling at a coral reef? Have you swum with the sweet fragrance of a summer flower meadow filling your nostrils? Or felt the power of the sea, bodysurfing a wave back to the shore? These are experiences you might never get any other way. It will help you understand nature, and as part of that, our place in the world.

24. To have constantly wet swim gear on rotation. Bathroom? No, that's my wetsuit-drying room, actually. (Remember not to hang it in the shower overnight or you risk having a heart attack on your half-asleep trudge to the toilet.) There's no feeling quite like sliding on a clingy, damp swimsuit, especially in the depths of winter. This takes out half the challenge of the swim: you are already a bit cold and wet, so get on with it and get in the water.

25. To develop your balance. Okay, there's that 'balance' you get within your mind, but I'm talking literal, physical balancing ability. You'll become adept at standing on one leg without a wobble as you pull on those dry socks. It takes time to master but is also a very good workout for your lower leg and ankle. Lots of tiny muscle movements are required to keep your foot planted and secure.

WHAT YOU SHOULD KNOW (26–71)

26. Knowledge and experience are more important than gear. You are constantly learning.

27. Don't say that outdoor swimming is a new 'thing' – people have been swimming outdoors for centuries.

28. 'Wild swimming' doesn't mean you are angrily doing the breaststroke.

29. Is outdoor swimming actually *wild?* It's not a term I use or like (full disclosure: I did previously use it), but we all see things differently: one person's 'wild swimming' may well be another's 'just swimming'. Swimming in a seaside Sydney lido and a mountain loch are both 'swimming' but one is more likely to be wilder than the other … I've been in Bronte Baths during a rough August swell! The term 'outdoor' covers a multitude of things, so to categorise one area of that with 'wild' helps people understand it, I suppose. I've taken part in races that took me on to wild, isolated islands, swum under icebergs in high mountain lochs and floated down long, bumpy rivers; each swim was outdoors, and each within itself required different experience, gear and techniques to survive. Don't get too bogged down trying to classify whether your swim is 'wild' or not – call it, or don't call it, what feels right.

30. We are all beginners at some point. Some of us pick up a skill as a child, others might not come to it until adulthood, but the fact remains: we are all new to swimming at some point in time.

31. You'll not be a marathon swimmer overnight. Fitness, breathing, technique, concentration and sighting (*tips 487–503*) are all things that take time to develop. Your body and mind will take time to adapt to new surroundings.

32. As you progress, swim in new conditions to push your boundaries.

33. Be responsible for yourself.

34. You'll probably get better as you get older. Don't try too much too soon.

35. A swim is often more of a mental challenge than a physical one. Believe you can do it and your body will follow.

36. Ignore the naysayers. There are lots of people in the world with opinions; if we listened to everyone's opinion of everything, nothing would get started.

37. Don't limit your ambition. Although you may come to swimming just to enjoy occasional dips, your goals may well develop and endurance may even become your thing. Don't ever doubt the changes you are capable of.

38. Follow your own path. Maybe you don't want to swim marathons; maybe you have no interest in head-up breast-stroke; you may hate the ice-cold water and a be a strictly warm-water person. Swim your own swim.

39. Stay curious: walk up that stream; go have a look at that beach; dunk your head to see what's under the surface.

40. Look to any opportunity to learn something new about water or swimming.

41. Respect other water users.

42. No snobbery, please. If someone enjoys the water in a different way to you, as long as it doesn't harm them or others, let them.

43. You don't need to post every swim on social media.

44. You don't need to post *any* swim on social media.

45. If you never posted your swim on social media, did you even swim?

46. Swimming outdoors satisfies the mind, body and soul.

47. Outdoor swimming is not what you do, it's who you are.

48. Some people swim all year in nothing more than togs and goggles, while others prefer to expose as little skin as possible to the water. Experiment and find what works for you: swim initially in a wetsuit, followed by a short dip in only a costume at the end of your session – this will help you to feel the difference between the two. Over time, adjust to what suits your body best.

49. Choose function over fashion.

50. You don't need a big changing robe in order to swim outdoors.

51. Finding your swim pod or tribe can be crucial. Swimming with others makes the sport more sociable and can help you stay motivated and become a better swimmer.

52. Be honest about your abilities, both with others and yourself.

53. Finding your own special spot is far more satisfying than swimming somewhere you've been told about.

54. Share knowledge, but be wary about who you share all your knowledge with. By that I mean don't tell everyone about your favourite swim spots; people will come to find it, and your special place might not be special any longer.

55. Get used to saying, 'Well, it depends … ' when people ask if outdoor swimming is safe.

Finding your swim pod can motivate you to become a better swimmer. © *Hannah Kettles*

56. Asking how long you should stay in the water is like asking the length of a piece of string. Equip yourself with the skills and experience to understand. The process of learning will take time. Be wary of giving a direct answer of 'X minutes' to strangers who ask for advice.

57. Don't follow any random 'X degrees Celsius means Y minutes in the water' formulas: the answer to how long you should be in for is entirely different for each swimmer. It's not a recipe on how to make a cake.

58. You don't need to put your head underwater. If it's not for you, it's not for you.

59. All bodies are different – people will react differently to the cold.

60. Reject peer pressure from children. If a 12-year-old can jump from the top of the tree into the river, it doesn't mean you have to … no matter how much their pals goad you.

61. 'It's positively tropical' means it's freezing cold.

62. 'Endolphins' are the endorphins you get from swimming. A classic line to drop to friends who question your decision to plunge into freezing waters.

63. 'Bioprene' is a euphemism for subcutaneous tissue that helps swimmers in cold water – also known as body fat.

64. You'll start to consider any body of water as a potential swim. Anything glimpsed from a train, plane, car or bike will give rise to the question, 'Could I swim in that?' If you give something a go and realise you have overestimated your abilities, take note and proceed with extra caution next time.

65. Swimming in rough water is worth mastering: it may be the most fun you ever have swimming. Rough water is water that is moving, often choppy and unpredictable. It may feel as though you are being thrown around in the water or slapped by waves. As you gain experience, water conditions that you consider to be 'swimmable' may become quite different to that of a non-swimmer.

66. The increase in outdoor swimming is like a wave. This wave is growing, but it's not yet started to break; in fact, it may still be the groundswell, growing in momentum. In time it may break, but rather than a solitary wave it may in fact be part of a set of waves: the best one is yet to come. To stretch this surf analogy even further, rather than a wave, we may be seeing a new 'break': where waves are consistently being produced. I always recommend looking at the Outdoor Swimming Society website for the latest information and advice from the community.

BASICS (1–194)

67. Become involved; we are all part of a wave. We need to urge governments to look after waters better, and companies and industries need to do better than they are doing. This will benefit nature and humans more widely. It's not just for us as swimmers, but we should care because it directly affects us.

68. Most people know absolutely zilch about swimming. Bear this in mind when hearing opinions from strangers, especially strangers who do not swim.

69. You may become addicted.

70. If you want an incredibly simple way of turning any dull day into a life-affirming adventure, just go for a swim.

71. You won't get any real experience from reading a book. Go swim.

SWIMMER'S LIFE (72–121)

72. What do you need to swim outdoors? In a word: nothing!

73. In a more considered way … it depends. From your swim aims and fitness to choice of location and group dynamics – there are many things to consider.

74. Many extra factors will affect what other 'stuff' you will or won't need for a swim: where you are, what your swim goals are, water temperature, how you react to the cold, your fitness, your group and other water users are all worth considering.

75. If you're planning a big or new swim, speak to someone who's done it or done similar.

76. Location choice for a swim is crucial for both enjoyment and safety. Every environment will have different challenges. Ask regular swimmers for safe places to swim.

77. Learn from others and use the knowledge of other swimmers. Time spent with experienced swimmers will help avoid many basic mistakes.

78. Learn to read maps. This can transform your appreciation of places and open up a world of discovery.

79. Check the weather forecast before you swim. Be prepared to change your plans.

80. Being a strong pool swimmer is a great start to swimming outdoors: good technique and fitness transfers over. However, there are many challenges to overcome and things to consider which won't arise in a pool.

81. You can practise open-water techniques and skills in the pool. Using a controlled environment to focus on nailing skills is useful for many swimmers.

82. Outdoor swimming is not the same as swimming in an indoor pool. You'll need new skills you don't use in the pool.

83. If you find your swimming skills are not what they used to be, or want to brush up on your abilities, find a qualified teacher.

84. Cold-water swimming is very different to cold-water immersion (a brief dunk in cold water, a cold shower or ice bath, where the focus is to embrace the cold rather than actually swim).

A secluded dunk.

85. Learn to make dynamic risk assessments. This will, in time, become a subconscious skill.

86. It's possible to float in only a few inches of water – this will come in handy.

87. Alcohol and water don't mix. If you've had a drink, your swim is done.

88. Keep your swimmers packed. Keep a swim kit in a small bag that you can slip into a backpack on any walk. My go-to is jammers (knee-length, tight-fitting shorts), a cap, goggles, earplugs and a thin hammam towel (a thin, lightweight towel that dries quickly in the sun).

89. Should you swim alone? In all honesty, I do swim alone, but not always. Swimming alone leaves you at far more risk if things go wrong: from the basics of losing a key and locking yourself out of a car to the dangers of the cold, injury or health issues in deep water. No person is invincible, and heading out on my own is a subject I find myself grappling with. The joy in a swim for me is often the freedom and feeling of having a place to myself – not having anyone else to answer to and not being restricted or controlled. I've made mistakes, I've learnt from experience and I've been in situations I'd never repeat. From mistakes experience grows, and lessons are learnt. To anyone taking up outdoor swimming – in whatever capacity – swimming alone is not something I would recommend.

90. I also go to the mountains alone. I walk and swim for multiple days on my own, not seeing another person. Maybe it's a misanthropic streak, maybe it's just within me to need to do it. But the more I do this, the more I think of safety. Should I always have someone with me if I want to swim to that island on a lake and explore? Should I come back to this river with a friend? If I'm honest, the urge to plunge in usually wins. Bear in mind that I have years of experience under my belt; never go out alone unless you are an experienced hiker and swimmer with a full understanding of the risks involved.

91. Remember to pee before getting in: cold water will make you need to go.

92. Take a bag for rubbish. I always try and pick up a few pieces and tidy up places, even if it's not my litter.

93. Wear old or comfy clothes to go swimming. Stuff will probably get wet and dirty.

94. Put your swimming stuff on at home – this can save a world of hassle.

95. Practise getting changed quickly in the summer. By the time it's winter, you'll be glad you did.

96. Wear something on your feet. Skin is no match for barnacles, rocks and glass.

97. Leave your clothes and things somewhere safe. If the tide is coming in, make sure it'll be above the high tide.

A day pack for a quick outdoor swim. I keep this packed for any walk or journey I take.

98. You don't have to indulge in specific breathing exercises prior to a swim, but don't discount it without trying it: it may be for you, it may not. Immediately before and while getting into the water I focus on deep, slow, controlled breathing, in through my nose and out through my mouth. The breaths out are controlled, with my mouth taking on a circular shape – it's an active process. Make sure not to puff as though you are blowing out a candle – it's much slower. Some people also like to go through sets of breathing and breath-holding exercises, such as the Wim Hof Method, prior to cold-water immersion.

99. In the UK, the water is generally some shade of cold most of the year. The coldest time tends to be from mid October until around April, but many factors affect this. A cold, wild winter will leave more snow on the hills which can keep rivers and lakes much chillier into summer. As warmer temperatures arrive, they will melt snow in the hills, leaving the run-off – especially rivers and streams – very cold.

100. Learn to pre-empt the cold. While on dry land, take a little gasp and allow yourself to feel a shiver move down your spine. This can help you deal with the initial cold. Imagine the pain as it creeps into your body; realise what is about to happen to you. It won't hit you in the same way as the water will, but it's a handy way to harden up your brain ahead of entry.

101. Don't judge a swim stroke by its splash. Some swimmers look like they're fighting the water, yet move quickly.

102. No matter what stroke you choose, focus on constantly breathing so that you are not holding your breath at any point. Keep your breathing smooth and steady, in time with your stroke, so that different points of your stroke will match up with your breath. For example, during breaststroke you may breathe out each time you reach forward with your arms. This may mean slowing down your swim stroke initially, but it will pay off in the long term.

103. Get your adrenaline rush fix by swimming straight into a jellyfish.*

104. If you don't like jellyfish, stay out of the sea.

* Possibly not the best idea.

Make sure you always know how to find your location, especially when seeking out secluded spots. © *John Weller @wildswimminglondon*

105. Don't swim with your electronic car key inside a flimsy plastic bag – double bag it, using sealed bags. I'll not explain why I know this. Options people use for a car key include leaving it on the wheel springs or using a Keypod to lock it in.

106. Dogs will pee on stuff left on the ground. Put your clothes in a bag, or above leg-cocking height.

107. Leave your stuff someplace safe. If you've got someone waiting on land, leave it with them. If it's a quiet, safe location then leave it in a bag hung on a tree. Alternatively, hide your valuables well or take them in your tow float.

108. Don't poo in the water.

109. Do not practise holding your breath on your own in the water.

110. Some outdoor swimmers employ drinking Coca-Cola as a method to prevent illness after a swim. Should you drink Coke after your swim? If you like Coke, go ahead. There's no scientific evidence it'll help an upset stomach though.

111. A little knowledge can be dangerous: just because you found one swim to be easy, it doesn't mean the next one will be.

112. Outdoor swimming can be used to commute or hold business meetings. If you live near a river, investigate whether you can swim to work. If you have a meeting, ask if they like to swim outdoors – if yes, you may have already sealed the deal.

113. Equip others with facts, not fear. Lots of information and even physical signs are based on the principle of keeping people out of the water entirely. This doesn't mean you should disregard signs – be aware of any danger they point out.

114. Learn to swim in winter: you're more likely to get the best places to yourself.

115. Water will drip out of your nose at an awkward time during your day. If you've been duck diving (diving underwater so you can go beneath a wave) or upside down in the water, expect this to happen later. After a swim, lean forward and hang your head between your legs to ease the water out.

116. 'Swimming skins' usually means swimming without a wetsuit, in a normal costume.

117. A swimskin, not to be confused with swimming skins, is a thin swimsuit that resembles a triathlon suit, but is not quite a wetsuit.

118. When taking a plane abroad, wearing your changing robe as a jacket is both space efficient and cosy. The large pockets allow for storage and their overall bulky size can take up your valuable luggage space.

119. Resist the urge to splurge on every single piece of gear. The chances are you'll not use half of them within a year.

120. Keep a spare towel in the car. You never know when the urge to swim will hit.

121. Remember to check your kit bag for old bananas that you forgot to eat.

GENERAL SAFETY (122–145)

122. Swim with others. Aside from other swimmers, it can be an entertaining spectator event for your partner or friends – unless you're doing a six-hour training swim, then it could be as much of an endurance event for them as it is for you. Always reward and thank your support crew.

123. Don't swim after heavy flooding or downpours. Unless you like swimming in excrement and mud.

124. If you are unable to swim, stay out of any water you don't know the depth of. It might seem basic, but shelves and sudden drops in depth where a step has been cut underwater have caused the deaths of people who were paddling and never intended to swim.

125. If you swallow water, stay calm. Stop swimming if it's safe to do so and tread water, facing away from any waves. Regain your breath. If you can stand or reach a safe place, do that too.

126. Stay hydrated – dehydration can lead to cramp. This includes having enough to drink before and after your swim.

127. Flex your legs occasionally. Calves and hamstrings can develop cramps during swims, especially over longer distances and in cold water. Every so often I will make sure to straighten my leg and flex my ankle towards my knee, to stretch the back of the leg. This will hamper your stroke as you do it, but it's better than cramp.

128. Cramp can be eased by floating and gently massaging the affected muscles.

Remember to wear water shoes in new environments.

129. Know who to call in an emergency. At sea call **999** and ask for the **coastguard**. On inland rivers or lakes call **999** and ask for **fire and rescue**.

130. Preregister your phone to be able to text 999 on EmergencySMS. This is useful in areas of weak or patchy signal. It's very simple: send the word '**register**' to 999. You will receive a text back, reply to this text with '**yes**'. In the event of an emergency, you can text 999 to tell them what emergency services you need, what the problem is and where you are.

131. Install the OS Locate app on your phone. This is a basic app that immediately gives you your location as a six-figure grid reference (based on GPS, not phone signal).

132. Other apps such as What3Words, while useful, can lead to problems: some word combinations sound very similar to others and there may be difficulty in the emergency services understanding a caller's accent and even mispronunciation of words, especially where phone signal might be weak.

133. Don't swim in blue-green algae blooms. Cyanobacteria, known as blue-green algae, occurs naturally in bodies of water and blooms in nutrient-rich, slow-moving water during periods of warm weather. It looks like a blue-green scum, pea soup or green lumps in the water, and swimming in it can cause illness or even rashes on the skin.

134. It's always best to heed signs about blue-green algae at swimming locations, but also remember that some signs are left up all year round, including when the water is fine to swim in and contains no blooms.

135. Keep your dog away from blue-green algae, as it can make them very ill.

136. Not all scum is dangerous. Decomposing plants and some algae will bloom into a non-toxic, brown, frothy scum, other algae (*Noctiluca scintillans*) can turn the water an orange colour and during the summer high pollen counts can create a yellow film on the surface. If you are unsure, don't swim.

137. Stand between large, wet rocks, not on top. You will go flying off them. Take care with your ankles.

138. Take it easy when moving on wet rocks. Keep your hands free of objects and move as though you are a gorilla: keep your knees soft and hands loosely by your side in case you need to use them.

139. Make yourself known to boat traffic, especially in areas where swimming is unusual. Use a tow float and bright cap or hat, and even shout to boats, 'Swimmer in water!' Smile and wave firmly (not frantically) and give way to faster craft. Be sure to get clear of their path.

140. Avoid swimming around jet skis.

141. If you hear an unusual, high-pitched whirr, it may be an outboard motor. Look up and assess where it is.

142. If a sign tells you that there's quicksand in an area, then there is.

143. Quicksand can move with the tide, and it won't always be in exactly the same place.

144. If you find yourself caught in quicksand, don't stand still and sink. Wiggle your limbs and try to lie down on to your back, spreading your surface area wider, and roll away. It's messy but it's better than being trapped.

145. Don't use pool inflatables outdoors. They're not designed for it and are swept away very quickly in the wind. If you are using them in a natural environment, choose a location where they can be kept under control and never rely on them as a safety device.

SAFETY OF OTHERS (146–161)

146. Ask how others feel before a group swim. Consider if they are happy, cold, nervous, stressed or focused. This is more important on swims that might require commitment, either in terms of distance, time away from land or challenging conditions.

147. If you are swimming as a group, take into account the weakest or slowest swimmers and consider making a schedule or swim that allows them to thrive. It might be that you can split a group into smaller groups of swimmers, with people of similar abilities and aims sticking together.

148. If you're swimming for the first time with someone, get to know them a bit. Ask about their experience and fitness, and be honest with others. Find out what they want to get from a swim.

149. Plan your swim, and swim your plan – but be prepared to change it.

150. Communicate with fellow swimmers; check how they are feeling as a swim progresses.

151. Keep communication straightforward. A simple, 'all good?' answered by a thumbs up or 'yes' can be enough most of the time.

152. Agree on hand gesture communication before entering areas where verbal communication is not possible. Reasons you can't hear well might be because of choppy water, loud environments like waterfalls or multiple swim caps and earplugs.

153. Stay close to each another, especially in choppy or moving water. You should be able to speak to one another.

154. Watch for any marked changes in swim speed and style in other swimmers – this could be an indication that someone is tiring and/or getting too cold.

155. Learn to spot drowning. Someone drowning usually makes no noise and is in an upright position, almost like treading water. They may bob up and down below the surface, with their head back, and may look like they are trying to climb a ladder or as if they are trying to doggy paddle.

156. Shout, reach, throw, row, go: this is the order in which to help someone if emergency services are not available. If you are safe and see someone in difficulty, shout to them. Give them clear instructions, such as telling them to grab a hold of something or to move to a safer location if possible. You may have an advantage of being in a position to see more than them, and will have a calmer mind. Shout for help if required. Reach for them if you are in a safe position, or use something that extends your reach that you can both hold, like a branch. Throw them a lifebuoy, ring or line. If a boat is available, use this to safely reach them in order to get them into the boat (if it is safe to do so) or use it to keep them afloat. Then go to them – this step should only be done if you know how to rescue someone, or you run the risk of the other swimmer pulling you under and putting you both in danger.

157. Swimming induced pulmonary edema (SIPE) is a condition where fluid collects in the lungs. It can be fatal and is triggered by swimming outdoors. Although it's still poorly understood, symptoms include coughing, pain or tightness in the chest and difficulty breathing. If you start to feel any of these symptoms, the current advice is to get out of the water as soon as possible; symptoms should recede once you are out of the water.

158. Early signs of hypothermia include 'the umbles', a series of telltale signs that progressively get worse. People will (usually) grumble, fumble, mumble, stumble and crumble in this order. The grumbles consist of moaning and negativity, fumbles are poor coordination and diminished motor skills, mumbles are slurred speech and the stumbles include tripping when moving and being unable to walk properly. If the person 'crumbles', they will lose the ability to walk and may become semi-conscious; this is now a life-threatening situation. Hypothermia will not occur suddenly but develop over time, so knowing what to look out for initially can help prevent it progressing.

159. Bear in mind that the above is not always easy to diagnose, especially if the swimmer is a grumpy, clumsy person generally.

160. If you do suspect that someone may be suffering from hypothermia, the focus should be on getting them warm and dry as soon as possible. After calling the emergency services, get any wet clothes off them, pat their skin dry and layer them up with dry clothes that will help them warm up, such as merino wool, thick, woolly jumpers and insulated jackets. Focus on getting their extremities warm, such as the head and hands. If possible, move them into a warm, dry environment.

161. Take snacks to share afterwards. Cake is always a winner – homemade cake for extra points (*tip 298*).

Remembering the snacks you brought for after your swim can help you to power through the last few minutes. © *John Weller @wildswimminglondon*

SWIMMING WITH CHILDREN (162–173)

162. Children often have great enthusiasm but less ability and experience to make the right judgements. Risk assess for them. Children, of course, vary wildly in their bravery and ambition, but very often won't take into account factors that are obvious to us – the strength of moving water being one.

163. If you are unsure about their swimming ability, use a buoyancy aid and wetsuit.

164. Plan for them. They often won't remember to bring enough layers to stay warm (I'm speaking from experience!).

165. They'll get cold before they know it. Enthusiasm might mask how cold they are, until all of a sudden they're shivering and have blue lips.

166. New and dynamic environments can be intimidating and very full on, so consider introducing them to a location before swimming: go for a picnic one day, throw stones the next day.

167. Choose a fun place to swim. They probably won't do that much swimming overall.

168. Keep to flat water, and avoid places with strong currents. Remember that even wading in water is much harder on smaller legs.

169. Ensure there is easy access: choose somewhere where you can walk in and out of the water easily, and where shallow water can be reached.

170. Avoid places with sudden underwater shelves. The sudden change from walking to swimming or floundering can lead to immediate panic, especially in inexperienced swimmers (this applies to adults too). A horrible experience around water can last many years in the memory and affect future behaviour.

171. Ask kids where's best to swim – they'll often find hidden gems and are a fount of knowledge. Given the right amount of freedom, children can make the very best local explorers: they'll find the exciting pools and the hidden waterfalls – the kind of places that make you feel like a child again.

172. Explore the world in a childlike way: take a walk down that path, peek around that next bay, see how deep that river pool is.

173. Don't force them into it, teach them to love it.

THE NASTY STUFF (ILLNESSES)
(174–176)

174. Swimmer's itch doesn't refer to the psychological itch that you may feel the need to scratch once you become addicted to outdoor swimming, but a skin rash caused by microscopic parasites which burrow into your skin. This is itchy and annoying and is best avoided by swimming away from areas where birds' nests and snails are found. Towel yourself dry vigorously as soon as you exit the water. The itchiness usually goes within a few days and corticosteroid cream or antihistamines can be used to reduce the itchiness.

175. Weil's disease. The urine of some animals, such as rats, mice, cows and dogs, carries a bacterial infection, leptospirosis, which can lead to Weil's disease – the signs are flu-like symptoms within around one to three weeks of exposure. To avoid this, cover any cuts or wounds before you swim, especially in urban or slightly dodgy water. Keeping hydrated and taking paracetamol can help reduce the symptoms, but if the symptoms develop it's worth consulting a medical practitioner as the disease can progress nastily.

176. Cryptosporidiosis/E. coli. Swimming in water contaminated with sewage or animal excrement can cause vomiting and diarrhoea. Avoid swimming near sewage outlets, don't swallow water while swimming and clean your hands thoroughly before eating.

PLANNING (177–184)

177. Some large inland waters have a lifeboat, either Royal National Lifeboat Institution (RNLI) or independently run. Keep this in mind if swimming in such a location.

178. Check the mobile signal coverage for where you're going.

179. If you're heading for a remote or adventurous swim, leave your route plan with someone you trust. Give them planned timings, locations and the contact details of any other group members. Have a plan with them that involves checking in on return, and then a set process to follow if they have not heard from you.

180. On some swims you'll need a safety vessel. Depending on the swim this could be a boat with an engine, a dinghy with an outboard, a stand-up paddleboard (SUP) or even a kayak. Safety vessels should be used for very long swims where fatigue may become a factor (especially if you're taking on your longest open-water distance swim), swims that are particularly committing in terms of environment (around a coastline with no safe exit points) or sea swims where tide and current or busy shipping channels will affect the swim. If you're taking on a long swim in an unfamiliar setting, consider whether you might benefit from some safety cover, even if this is just from experienced, confident paddlers who can act as your eyes and ears with a better vantage point. They can also carry your snacks!

181. Find the right boat and safety crew. Use experienced water people and a crew you trust, and if possible train and practise with them. For example: understand how to hold on to a kayak if you need help, set out how you intend to communicate with one another and establish what will happen in emergency situations.

182. Some boat safety crews are expensive. Find out their costs and consider if you can ask experienced people you know instead; but also consider the different levels of safety and experience on offer.

Be prepared to change your plans according to the weather, even if conditions look calm.

Avoid choppy conditions if you are still learning to swim outdoors.

BASICS (1–194)

183. Give your team your plan. Have a written plan with your feed times, estimated speed, any specific communication requirements and inspiring snippets/heckling motivation. Having a main point of contact on the boat who knows you well is a huge help.

184. Have any kit that you'll need in clear boxes, clearly labelled, and group by similar stuff.

WEATHER (185–194)

185. Get used to checking the weather regularly. Met Office, XC Weather and WillyWeather are three of my favourite websites to use. When heading for swims in the English, Scottish or Welsh mountains, use the Mountain Weather Information Service (MWIS).

186. Pay close attention to the wind. This is the biggest weather variable for swimming and can entirely change your swim, preparation and recovery.

187. If the wind forecast is high, look for a sheltered swim. Think about the wider geography of the location: wide bays facing the open sea are susceptible to waves.

188. Check overhead in strong winds – trees and branches can be brought down easily.

189. Get changed out of the wind. Spend as little time as possible in the wind both before and after your swim. Being wrapped in neoprene is a big help here.

190. Offshore wind is when the wind is blowing from land out to sea. An onshore wind is the opposite: from sea to land.

191. If the wind is blowing in the opposite direction to the tidal flow, it throws up small, choppy, awkward waves and is known as wind over tide, making swimming challenging.

192. If you are still learning to swim outdoors, avoid choppy conditions.

193. Make sure to swim at least a few times in the rain – you may get hooked. It's the perfect time to view the water at surface level and see the patterns as the drops dance.

194. Stay out of the water during thunderstorms.

Always consider underwater shelves or rocks before getting in.

002

THINGS TO CONSIDER (195–270)

'Believe that you are meant to be here, and even talk to yourself out loud. I regularly indulge in a self-pep talk — it can really put things into perspective.'

Take time to take in your surroundings.   © *John Weller @wildswimminglondon*

THINGS TO CONSIDER (195–270)

FEAR, ANXIETY AND DEEP WATER
(195–208)

195. If you feel fear about a swim, try and identify what exactly scares you. It might not even be about the actual swim, but something else. Sometimes even a popular swimming location can feel 'wrong' to some people.

196. Fear is normal. It's often a response to something unknown, or the effects of a previous bad experience. Try and put it into context: can you think of a similar situation you were scared of and then overcame?

197. Build up to it: spend longer periods in water you feel comfortable in, then take a short swim in deeper water. Swim just outside your comfort zone and see how it goes.

198. There are a variety of ways to help you deal with deep water fear. Remember, there is no giant squid – wait, don't think about giant squid!

199. Control your breathing: actively focus on keeping a steady, regular rhythm. You might need to slow your swimming down at first, but this is probably a good thing in the long term.

200. If you don't like putting your face in for front crawl, practise in the shallows: while standing in waist-deep water, bend forward and adopt the swimming position with your top half. Practise breathing and arm movement without actually swimming, and complete 20–30 strokes. Take a break and recover your breath fully, then repeat the process, completing two to three sets. That might be all you try for the day, as front-crawl breathing is a skill that can take time to master.

201. Break it down into shorter chunks. Think of the next 20 strokes and count them out. Take the chance to reset and go for 20 more. Before you know it, you've done 100 strokes and the focus required has taken your mind off other things.

202. If you can swim, just keep swimming. It's like a pool: your body is doing mostly the same things. That's all you're doing: swimming.

203. The power of positivity: what you think directly impacts how you feel and behave. Believe that you are meant to be here, and even talk to yourself out loud. I regularly indulge in a self-pep talk – it can really put things into perspective.

204. If you have a bad or frightening swimming experience, tell someone about it. Talk it through, try and place it in context. Understand what went wrong and how to avoid that in future.

205. After scares, ease yourself back with gentle swims and positive swimmers.

206. Book a personal session with an experienced coach. Having someone who is there specifically to help you and talk you through the process can be a paradigm-shifting experience.

207. Remember a positive swim. What was it that made you feel so good? Put yourself back in that place and think about that experience being repeated on your swim today.

208. A swim is a swim. Once you can't touch the bottom, does it matter how much deeper it is? Remember that you will float.

Be careful not to disturb birds or wildlife. © John Weller @wildswimminglondon

ANIMALS (209–232)

209. Don't fear wildlife. Seals, for example, can be very curious and playful creatures and may follow you from a distance to snort and sniff, or even come for a close-up look. If a seal does approach you, do not try to interact with them – you may distress them if you do.

210. Wildlife is generally benign. Nothing is out to actively get you but entering into new environments will always pose new risks.

211. Don't disturb birds or animals.

212. Avoid sensitive areas. Pay attention to local guidance, especially during bird nesting season and when wildlife are raising young – this might include accessing a swim location. Riverbanks, islands and areas of long grass can all be home to a variety of birds and animals.

213. Tread lightly on sandy banks – they may be home for burrowing birds and animals.

214. Give geese and swans lots of space: they can be aggressive and won't take any of your rubbish. In late summer they may be extra protective of cygnets.

215. Let sleeping seals be. Don't approach them on rocks and keep at least 100 metres away from them.

216. Don't feed wild animals in their environment. It may be tempting to get an Instagram banger of that old red deer who now hangs around the car park, but consider if it's right for the animal and safe for you. Animal behaviour changes throughout the year, meaning they may be aggressive towards humans during different seasons. Reliance on irregular human feeding can also lead to health and behaviour changes that could put an animal at risk.

217. Stay calm in any interaction and try to avoid any sudden movements. If you keep relaxed and in control of yourself, it usually results in a better interaction for all.

218. Keep interactions on an animal's terms: let them come to you if they want to and don't seek them out for close encounters, especially if you are on their territory.

Check the water conditions of anywhere you're planning to swim.
© John Weller @wildswimminglondon

219. Learn what jellyfish are in your local waters. Around the UK, lion's mane, Portuguese man-o-war and mauve stingers are usually the only ones to worry about, and they won't be in all places at all times. Lion's manes can become populous in summer, while seeing a Portuguese man-o-war is rare. The deadliest jellyfish in the world are the box jellyfish family, found mainly in tropical and subtropical waters. The tiny Irukandji, found in Australian waters, are often considered one of the most poisonous jellyfish to humans.

220. Where safety measures are in place, follow them. In Queensland in Australia, many beaches have designated swimming areas set up, encompassed by a stinger net. These are large nets that sit in the water, held up by a floating boom, and are designed to keep out box jellyfish. Consider also using a Stinger Suit™ (effectively a Lycra onesie) if you're in the sea during stinger season.

221. Where you see one jellyfish, expect to see more.

222. Some jellyfish don't sting at all, while others can have very nasty, if not life-threatening, stings.

223. Don't pee on a jellyfish sting. Unless you like being peed on.

224. Rinse jellyfish stings in seawater, remove any tentacles and soak the sting area in the hottest water you can bear. Leave stings open and uncovered. Fresh water can cause the stinging cells to fire off, so using something acidic such as vinegar helps neutralise cells and stop further stinging.

225. In my experience, jellyfish will rise to the surface and become more abundant in calm, settled, warm waters.

226. Jellyfish appear to be influenced by moon phases, with research suggesting that swarms appear just before and during full moons. In my experience, a calm summer evening during a full moon can be one of the most relaxing and uplifting times to swim in the sea – but also to spot jellyfish.

227. It is very unlikely that you will see jellyfish throughout the winter in the UK.

228. Take care around farm animals: cows are very curious, might follow you and might even block you getting out of the water.

229. Avoid swimming downstream from animal-intensive farms, especially after heavy rain. By-products of agriculture such as manure may be washed off the land into waterways by rain. Wet ground and heavy rain can also lead to animals falling into rivers, dying and decomposing there. I have had to remove the carcass of a sheep from upstream of what was my favourite small river pool. Avoiding swims after heavy rainfall also applies to areas where chemicals such as pesticides and herbicides are sprayed on to crops.

230. Keep an eye out for ticks: they are prevalent in summer and can carry Lyme disease. Remove them as soon as you find them using a tick-specific tool, or tweezers if you don't have one. Make sure to remove the head and keep an eye on the bite mark; if it turns into a bullseye mark, see a doctor. Wearing trousers and long sleeves helps keep ticks off, as well as dark-coloured clothing – but this also makes them harder to spot when they do get on your clothes.

231. Summer is midge/midgie season in the Scottish Highlands. These minuscule flying insects bite, and although they don't carry disease they can send you into fits of rage. They are at their worst in the West Highlands, in peaty, heathery terrain. Avon Skin So Soft and Smidge are the two best products, in my experience, to deal with them. Cover your skin and wear a midge net, with a wide-brim hat underneath to keep it off your face. They won't follow you far off the shore, so get in the water!

232. Fish and eels will be more afraid of you than you are of them.

BIOSECURITY (233–242)

233. As swimmers we have a responsibility to take care of our environment – this means how we get to locations, what we do while we're there and how we leave it after we've been.

234. Try and avoid the transfer of any contamination or potentially invasive species between bodies of water. Follow the guidance of Check Clean Dry.

235. Check your clothing and anything that'll be in the water for organisms or plant material. Check awkward spots like zips, seams and the bottom of shoes. Do this before and after your swims.

236. After a swim, clean all your gear thoroughly once you get home. Rinse it well in a bucket of fresh water and empty that into the garden or ground, rather than straight down the drain. If you swim regularly, having a big bucket of rainwater or fresh water in the garden can be handy.

237. Dry all your kit fully before you use it again.

Spread the word about biosecurity, even if you have to do it during a swim.

238. All the previous points should also be followed for support craft like SUPs, kayaks, paddles and anything that enters the water.

239. If taking on a multiple-swim trip, you could change your gear as you change between bodies of water. For example, carrying two or three swimsuits will reduce the risk of accidentally transferring contamination between bodies of water.

240. If your swims are all within the same catchment area, consider multiple swims that head in the same direction as the water flow. Start at the source and head downstream.

241. Follow local rules – some areas have specific problems with invasive species. This is particularly important in bodies of fresh water and especially in some areas of the Lake District in England, with signs and campaigns highlighting issues such as the spread of New Zealand pigmyweed.

242. Spread the word and encourage others to do the same. Biosecurity issues are not yet that well known among swimmers, but with its relatively new popularity we have the chance to get it right early on.

IS IT CLEAN? (243–254)

243. If the water looks disgusting, it probably is.

244. If it smells bad, it probably is. Use your common sense. In fact, use all your senses apart from your taste – there's no need for that. It's not uncommon for water to get into your mouth during a swim, so if you do taste something 'off', don't swallow it.

245. Some bodies of water naturally contain few nutrients (they are referred to as oligotrophic or dystrophic) so despite appearing somewhat empty or devoid of life, they can be very clean to swim in. Waters like this are generally unlikely to see algal blooms. But just because they are devoid of nutrients it doesn't necessarily mean the water will be clear: they can be peaty. Oligotrophic lakes usually contain clear water and are found in cold regions of the world. They can also be identified by a lack of flora or fauna within the water and are often deep.

246. A vibrant ecosystem with biodiversity is usually a good sign that water is clean. Look for wildlife or evidence of wildlife: birds, dragonflies, flowers and fish.

247. It might not be immediately easy to find information on a location. Asking local swimmers is often the quickest way to investigate whether it's suitable for a swim; asking on online swim forums or groups will often give you an idea of how suitable a location is. Try and be clear in the information you seek, such as asking about one area of a larger lake, and be specific about your plans. Bear in mind that some spots, even if they look great, may carry connotations or a strength of feeling within a local community, for example where accidents have occurred in the past.

248. Sadly, many of the bodies of water in the UK – especially in urban settings – are not swimmable, or at least not safely: raw sewage gets pumped into seas and rivers, and this is even worse after heavy rainfall.

249. The UK's devolved environmental agencies and the Environmental Protection Agency in Ireland monitor water quality at a limited number of designated bathing waters, but only during the bathing water season, which is often classed as May or June to September.

250. Take care in rivers that pass by areas of farmland, as they can be polluted by agricultural run-off.

251. Surfers Against Sewage have a very useful interactive water quality map, highlighting when sewage is released into coastal and some inland waters. However, not all of the information is available all-year round.

252. The Rivers Trust have a hugely detailed interactive map that shows the location of sewage overflows in England and Wales as well as the discharges of treated sewage into rivers from the last year. Avoid swimming just downriver of these discharges.

253. After a swim, wash your hands before eating.

254. Test the oft-reported 'immune-system-boosting effects of wild swimming' by taking a long soak in the River Thames right after a downpour.*

JUMPING (255–270)

255. Never make a jump your very first entry if you don't know your body of water and/or the water is cold.

256. Always make sure water is deep enough before jumping in.

257. Generally, the higher the jump the deeper the water needs to be.

258. The easiest way to test water depth is to swim directly to where you aim to hit the water and duck dive down, feeling with your hands and having a look around. You can also use a stick or, if you're keen, an avalanche probe to test depth.

* Don't actually.

Make sure you are jumping away from any water features or rocks. © *John Weller @wildswimminglondon*

259. There is no exact formula for how deep you will go when jumping into water. Your depth will be affected by factors such as your weight, your style of jump (pencil, bomb or dive), whether you wear a wetsuit and whether you bend underwater once submerged.

260. If it's a body of water that's liable to change, such as a river or the sea, then checking for hidden dangers is even more important. Currents will move trees and debris and shift sandbanks or even rocks.

261. Make sure you are jumping away from any water features that could trap you underwater. Many river pools are inviting but can contain dangers such as undertows (underwater currents that move in the opposite direction to any surface current) or undercut rocks (essentially underwater caves that you cannot see).

262. If you swim in a canal or near a residential area, rascals will throw shopping trolleys into the water. Canals, especially near road bridges, are a classic spot for items to be chucked in – they are a magnet fisher's dream.

263. Check what's underfoot before any dive or jump, especially if jumping from a natural environment. Check that the surface is solid and won't crumble or cause you to slip. You can never be 100 per cent sure of the strength of an overhanging rock or vegetation, and changes in environmental factors can affect this.

264. Learn to dive with correct form: your head should be in a neutral, normal position. Don't look ahead at the water – many a pair of goggles have been lost this way.

265. As a rule, when jumping in from a height your body position should be vertical upon entry, your head facing forward (don't look directly down at the water), feet together and arms close to your body; a favoured position is fists in front of the face, elbows down and arms together. During the fall, you may naturally 'wind down the windows' with your arms to keep balance and body position – pull them into the correct position for entry. Better this than jumping like a rigid frozen sausage that overbalances for a classic 'slap' entry.

266. Jumping into water is a skill. Like any skill, you can develop and improve over time by practice and through tuition from more skilful practitioners. Taking a canyoning or gorge-walking course is a great way to learn about both water hazards and jumping techniques, with a particular focus on moving water in river settings.

267. If you don't want to do it, don't. Peer pressure won't help you fix an injury.

268. Step, don't always jump. If you're at a ledge, choose your landing spot, look ahead and step out on to it.

269. Don't jump in with a tow float attached, unless you like to be hoicked back up to the surface inelegantly or want some rope burn.

270. Howl like Tarzan. Or squeal. Or roar. Externalise fear and expel it from your body.

Prepare to go straight into your recovery routine as soon as you leave the water. © John Weller @wildswimminglondon

003

THE SWIMMER'S BODY (271–391)

*'Faffing before a swim seems almost like a prerequisite,
and for many swimmers is a part of their preparation;
faffing after a swim is precious time lost.'*

A serene swim in High Dam in the Lake District, England. © *Jumpy James*

Disprove the myth that you can't eat before swims by eating *during* a swim.

PIE? CAKE? HOT CHOCOLATE? ... NUTRITION (271-291)

271. Outdoor swimming is a sport in which eating copious amounts of calories can be of benefit to performance!

272. Increasing your body fat gives you extra insulation and buoyancy.

273. Ever heard you shouldn't eat anything just before a swim? Not true – you'll even have to eat *during* some swims.

274. But do avoid large meals just before swimming – give your body the time to digest it.

275. As long as you've fuelled beforehand, you shouldn't need to eat on a swim that's around two hours or less.

276. If you're going to eat during a swim, always practise, practise and practise again with that food and method of fuelling during training sessions.

277. Nutrition on long swims is a very personal thing. Some swim foods that I find work well are bananas, flat coke, energy chews, energy gels, chocolate, jelly babies, canned peaches and Mars bars.

278. Opinions vary on how often you should eat on long swims, from anything between 15 to 45 minutes. I like something around the 35-minute mark.

279. Your tongue might get irritated by the salt water on long sea swims, so choose something that's easy to chew and swallow.

280. Once you nail it and find what works for you, train with the same meal.

281. My go-to breakfast – several hours before swimming – is hot porridge. A large bowl supplemented with a banana, nuts, seeds and a large dollop of peanut butter as a protein source is a simple meal, and I can usually source it or make it most places I go, even if I'm camping.

282. Tuck thin bars or gels inside a tight swimsuit or wetsuit.

283. Wetsuit arms and legs are the easiest places to stash food.

284. Keep bars in one arm, empty wrappers in the other. This will stop them going into the water or causing confusion.

285. Have something you like handy. Sometimes you need that psychological lift from eating a bag of gummy bears.

286. The swimming position can trigger gastric reflux – some sports drinks bring it on really badly for me. To deal with it, change to an upright position and ride out the pain – taking water and indigestion tablets also helps. If you identify a food that causes this, try and avoid using it.

287. The most common way to fuel for marathon swimmers is by using a mixed carbohydrate drink like Maxim or CarboPro.

288. If you're being fed from a boat, make sure everyone knows how it will work: will it be given to you on a line or pole?

289. Should you drink the water? Only if you're sure that it's clean. I've sipped as I swam through lochs and rivers in the Highlands of Scotland, but only in remote areas away from any houses, industry or animals. This does save time. Clear, flowing water is recommended over still or coloured water, but colour may just be staining from peat – some houses have safe, brown water coming from the taps!

290. Be wary of sipping water you're unsure about. I once got a rancid stomach from drinking straight from a stream in an area where sheep graze. I suspect it was a dead sheep floating somewhere upstream, however it may also have been from swimming across the Firth of Forth and taking a couple of involuntary mouthfuls of the water a couple of days previously.

291. Use a straw or filter to be even safer. This is not a paper drinking straw you get from a fast-food outlet, but a larger drinking straw that contains a hollow filter or series of tubes which helps remove bacteria and dirt as water is drawn through it. A less awkward option is to get a water bottle with a built-in filter, which acts in the same way. Another option is to use water purification tablets, such as chlorine tablets. Placed in a bottle of water, they usually take around 30 minutes to act, killing most waterborne viruses and bacteria. This can be combined with neutralising tablets if you're not too keen on the taste of chlorine.

RECOVERY FOOD (292–304)

292. Eat after a swim. Your body will need the fuel. It's also one of the best ways to help yourself get back to 'normal'.

293. Start with something easy to eat that provides instant energy.

294. Your main recovery meal should be a mixture of carbohydrate and protein to help repair your body. Have a protein shake and try and eat within an hour of a training swim or a particularly intensive swim.

295. Your jaw may struggle to deal with chewy things when cold, so go for soft foods.

296. Mars bars, Snickers and other chocolate left in the cold will turn rock solid – keep them wrapped up.

297. Cake is always a clear favourite among swimmers. Debate rages on over which cake, or even biscuit, is the best.

298. For me, the winner might be lamingtons. An Australian classic, they are a sponge cake dipped into chocolate icing and coconut. This is my grandmother's recipe, passed down to my mother and now to you!

Preparation: 60 minutes (30 minutes prepping, 30 minutes cooking). Makes 12.

To make the sponge
400g self-raising flour
150g granulated sugar
125g butter
3 eggs
120ml milk
Vanilla essence
Pinch of salt

To make the icing
260g icing sugar
4tbsp cocoa powder
125g butter
1tsp lemon essence
Warm water
200g desiccated coconut

- Set your oven to 180 °C (gas 4).
- Sift the flour and salt together.
- Cream the sugar and butter. Add the eggs and vanilla essence.
- Beat well, then fold in the flour and salt and add the milk.
- Grease a lamington tin (or similar rectangular shallow baking dish) and pour in the mixture.

- Bake at 180 °C for 30–35 minutes, then allow to cool on a wire rack.
- Once the cake is cool, cut it in half and then cut into 12 squares.
- Make the icing by sifting the icing sugar and cocoa powder together.
- Melt the butter then add the lemon essence and beat this mixture into the icing sugar and cocoa.
- Beat well, adding enough water to give the required smooth consistency.
- Dip each lamington into the icing. Use skewers to allow excess icing to drip off the lamingtons before rolling in the coconut.
- Roll them in the coconut (in a wide bowl) while the icing is still moist. Coconut can get very messy – use a small amount at first rather than all at once.
- An upgrade is to spread jam over each lamington before dipping it into the icing.
- Enjoy!

299. A warm drink will help raise your spirits. Holding a warm cup also helps you warm your hands, but shivers and shakes can mean the drink spilling all over the place. A good solution is filling a large cup halfway, instead of filling a small cup up to the brim. Hot chocolate or a hot sweet drink helps. Sip on your drink, but don't down it immediately.

300. Try sugar. I hate sugar in hot drinks, unless I've been swimming in the cold – then I love it.

301. Forget faffing with an AeroPress or moka pot at the water's edge – just use a flask.

302. Emergency chocolate is vital – keep some in your swim bag.

The moment you realise you've got lamingtons for your post-swim snack.

303. Avoid alcohol if you're cold – wait until you've warmed up again. Once you've had any alcohol, that's your swimming done.

304. Having said that, having a quick nip of whisky after a cold dook – maybe a short dunk more than a 'proper' swim – is a sensational feeling.

GETTING IN AND GETTING OUT
(305–315)

305. Every swimmer you meet will have their own tricks and techniques that work for them – not all will work for you.

306. Don't overthink it – say you're getting in and commit to it.

307. Walk in. Take the time to feel the cold on different parts of your body. For me it's a different sensation, both physically and mentally, as the water reaches new areas. First are the feet, where sheer pain and doubt kicks in; the crotch-to-belly-button area brings slight shock, and willpower is required; nipples bring pain and facial contortion, and a deep, deliberate breathe out is required; finally, when the water reaches my shoulders joy and relief arrive, as well as thoughts of *ah, well, that wasn't so bad, was it?!*

308. Be brave and confident as you enter the water. Stride or move with purpose, rather than shuffling (if it's safe underfoot). You are going to get cold – this can't be avoided.

309. Splash water on your face and neck. This can stimulate the vagus nerve and your body will anticipate the cold to come.

310. If you are entering from a ladder, hold yourself on it for 30 seconds once you are immersed, to help you get over any initial fear.

311. When you're barefoot on stones, be like a frog … by this I mean stay low for as long as possible. Even when it's no longer deep enough to swim, it's possible to float and pull yourself over rocks to the shore. I have done this to just a few centimetres of water depth. Numb feet on cold rocks are a horrible experience, and it can take a long time to walk a short distance.

312. Stony ground, especially where there may be a walk to deep water, can be excruciating. Wearing neoprene socks or water shoes helps a lot, but water shoes will cause drag during actual swimming.

313. One solution is to wear thin sandals or Crocs that can be attached on to a tow float during your swim, and you then have them handy for the exit.

314. Another option that works for floating footwear is to have them attached by a long string to something heavy, like a stone or diving weight. Once you have reached the right depth, slip them off. You can then swim back to them for your exit. The shoes float, like a buoy, with the stone/weight as the mooring on the seabed. If you go for this set-up, keep the weight on a string and use a small karabiner to loop through the footwear.

315. Where there is a current, your shoes may move or disappear.

RECOVERY (316-357)

316. What you do after a swim, especially a cold swim, is even more important than what you do beforehand. Getting your recovery process nailed down is crucial.

317. If you get your recovery wrong, you could end up feeling cold or rough all day.

318. Get changed in five minutes – any longer than that and you're just faffing.

319. Plan ahead and take into account the time it takes to recover and warm up, especially from a cold swim.

320. The aim is to warm up gradually. Do not immediately get into a warm shower or bath after a particularly long, cold or gruelling swim. One December many years ago, I almost passed out in a warm shower within a few minutes of a cold 800-metre swim.

321. Understand the after-drop, the process by which your core temperature continues to drop after you exit the water and you are basically still cooling down. This occurs around 10–30 minutes post-swim. It has been attributed to cold blood from your extremities returning to your core, but further studies suggest that the cold is actually still moving through you – a process of conduction.

322. Dry yourself thoroughly but don't rub or massage the skin if you're very cold.

323. Dry between your toes properly. Your body will be losing heat by evaporation, so the aim is to get your skin dry and not cause your body to work harder than necessary itself. This also helps to prevent the damp environment in which athlete's foot and dry skin can develop. Take care not to damage cold toes by rubbing gently.

324. Look after your hands. When it's cold, don't leave them wet – make sure to dry them properly, then keep them protected. If you don't, you run the risk of the skin drying out, cracking and causing painful bleeding, especially around the nails and knuckles. Apply hand cream at night – I swear by O'Keeffe's Working Hands.

325. Keep out of the wind. Use any shelter available, whether that be trees, buildings or a pop-up tent. The difference between getting changed and recovered on a wild day compared to a calm one is huge.

326. Accept help from your supporters. Your motor functions reduce in the cold: your speech may be slurred, your decision making will be affected and you won't be able to judge temperatures easily on cold skin.

327. Make sure you're not being given a piping hot drink, as your reduced ability to evaluate temperatures may mean you burn yourself. A large temperature difference between a hot liquid and cold tissue can also cause scalding. Your supporters should know to test it themselves.

328. Disregard silver foil blankets – they will not help you. These blankets are designed to reflect radiated heat, however a cold swimmer's body radiates very little heat. They provide very little in terms of insulation and when placed against bare skin will conduct heat away, cooling a swimmer down – the opposite of what's needed.

329. Changing robes help.

330. There are a huge variety of designs of changing robes, from basic towelling ones to the larger wind resistant and waterproof designs that are effectively like a giant, hooded trench coat. Many popular designs won't actually dry you, but more offer protection from the elements, a hidden place to change your clothes and an excellent outer layer for standing around in.

331. Wear your changing robe when shopping to save on bags: the pockets are huge. They are also ideal for bad-weather dog walking.

332. Have your clothes ready, the right way up and organised. Faffing before a swim seems almost like a prerequisite, and for many swimmers is a part of their preparation; faffing after a swim is precious time lost.

333. Wrap your clothes around a hot water bottle. It's a great psychological boost, and you can then tuck the bottle inside your layers.

334. Choose clothes without fiddly buttons or awkward zips: cold hands are no good at buttons.

335. Layer up your clothing. Start with something that is easy to slip on – I like a thin merino woollen layer – for both your top and bottom halves, followed by a T-shirt, jumper or two, an insulated jacket and finally a windproof outer layer. Also put on a thick hat and gloves.

336. Wear jogging bottoms and avoid denim: it doesn't retain warmth and is rubbish when wet.

337. Having a base layer on creates warmth and insulation, and baggier clothing on top then means you're not losing body heat immediately to the atmosphere.

338. Don't bother with underwear. They can be a nightmare to get on after a swim, and putting on a spare swimsuit is often much easier.

339. Dress your top half first. Once you are fully layered up on top, switch your focus to your legs and feet.

340. Cold-water swimming can lead to a sort of tunnel vision, whereby you can become focused on one task to the detriment of other stuff. Don't become fixated on getting your socks just right.

341. Stand on something, as your feet will lose heat to the ground. Make it something comfortable – I've used old carpets, bath mats, spare jackets and bags.

342. An extravagant option is to take a basin and flask of warm water (not hot) to stand in. I find this to be very pleasant and it helps me relax a bit more in what can be a stressful time.

343. Consider using shoes that are too big, or slip-on sandals. If you have two or three pairs of socks on, your normal shoes might not fit. Your hands might not be able to handle laces either.

344. Swap your laces for triathlon/bungee laces: they are much quicker and easier to tie with cold hands.

345. Once dressed, consume a warm drink and a snack. I like sugary foods that don't require too much chewing, such as cake or a Snickers bar – make sure they're not left out in the cold. Your body will appreciate the calories, and although the drink doesn't really warm you up it's a great psychological boost.

346. A warm environment can help recovery, such as a heated vehicle or even a warm (not hot) sauna – if you've got heated car seats, use them. Remember that these are warming the skin, rather than your core – it's bringing your core temperature back to normal that is the main focus.

347. Once fully dressed and feeling okay, I like to move around in a fairly gentle way. Usually this just means an easy walk, maybe swinging some gentle air punches at nearby branches, or invisible foes. This will help generate body heat.

348. Shivering is natural and not to be feared: this is the body warming up. Shivering also uses up fuel – another reason to snack.

349. It's natural to feel sleepy a few hours after recovering from a cold swim.

350. The whole process of outdoor swimming and recovery is hard on the body – make sure to get plenty of rest if swimming in the cold over multiple days.

351. Don't panic if your fingers go pale or white: many swimmers suffer from Raynaud's disease, a phenomenon which affects blood flow. This usually shows in the fingers. For many people it is a cost of cold-water swimming and does not stop them.

352. To quickly warm cold hands, stick them under your armpits or against the base of your throat.

353. Help others get warmed up: face each other, hold hands with palms up and push/pull opposite arms. Speed it up and continue until you can't; it's fun and will help warm you up.

354. A positive mindset always helps. If you tell yourself you're cold and miserable, you will be. You can be cold, but you don't have to be miserable.

355. Don't wear your base layers indoors once you're warmed up. This might sound unusual and may even be highly specific to me, but I find once I'm warmed up and back indoors that having base layers on causes me to become very irritable and annoyed by the simplest things. This usually happens an hour or two after a swim. It might be simply that I'm overheating, but recognising this and swapping to a cotton T-shirt and shorts usually solves it instantly.

356. Practise and refine your rewarming and recovery process. Don't be afraid to try new ideas.

357. Do not try to drive until you are fully recovered.

If it's possible (and safe) to swim with your dog, always swim with your dog. © *John Weller @wildswimminglondon*

Invest time into learning about your cycle so you can tailor your swims around your needs. © *John Weller @wildswimminglondon*

MENSTRUAL CYCLE* (358–368)

358. Despite being a grown woman who has had periods for more than half of my life, I still get it wrong and can struggle to deal with the 'ick' factor when I am in the outdoors and swimming wild. Here are some of my top tips for managing your period as an outdoor swimmer.

359. Track your cycle. Using an app has made a huge positive change in how I view my menstrual cycle. It took me from *what the hell is wrong with me?* to *oh, phew, it's just my period*. Once you have logged enough data and the app learns about your cycle, you can plan outdoor activities with reasonable confidence. There are lots of free apps; mine sends alerts to remind me to log data or let me know that my period is due. Using an app has helped me tackle symptoms like lower back pain: I learnt that increasing my level of activity in the days leading up to my period led to reduced pain and more energy. Your symptoms and how you deal with them will vary; the important thing is investing time to learn about your cycle.

360. You might find your body runs hotter or colder during your period, and this should be factored in when planning swims and outdoor activities. You might need to take more layers to wear or reduce your time in the water. Many people who have periods experience low energy and low mood during their period, and while gentle exercise may help relieve symptoms, you might need to save longer and more strenuous swims until your period has finished.

361. You can take a course of tablets (norethisterone) to delay your period. It's not something I do on a regular basis, maybe once every few years, and I've found this handy when I have been on work trips where I know my schedule will be very intense or when I'm trekking in a very hot or very cold country. These tablets are available from chemists, but you should discuss it with your GP first.

362. Using a menstrual cup is a great way to be environmentally friendly during your period. After the initial investment it usually works out cheaper than disposable products in the long term. Carry a bottle of water to wash it out and make sure your hands are clean before and after use. I'm yet to perfect emptying and replacing a cup while outdoors and usually switch to period pants after removing my cup.

363. Invest in period pants – there are plenty of affordable options now including period swimwear. I find period pants are the best solution for me post-swim, even on heavy days. Our body pressure changes in the water, slowing the flow of your period and making it feel like your period has been temporarily paused. You may choose to swim without any period protection and that's okay. It's unlikely you will leak a trail of blood behind you, and even if you do, it's a myth that sharks can sense a woman on her period!

364. Traditional sanitary towels and tampons are not considered the most environmentally friendly choice, but they might be the most practical thing for you, and plastic-free options are widely available. I carry doggy bags or a clip-lock box to carry out period waste and tissues. Always make sure you remove and/or change your tampon after swimming, as they absorb water.

365. Did you know a rinsed-out, cotton tampon makes a great firelighter? I put them through the wash with my reusable sanitary pads and period pants. I pondered if sharing this tip was a step too far, but a deep dive into the internet told me that menstrual blood can be used in many ways, from fertiliser to face masks, so I guess I'm not that odd after all.

* Thank you to Suzanna Cruickshank, outdoor swim guide and author of *Swimming Wild in the Lake District*, for contributing this section.

366. Make yourself a hygiene pack. It's handy to carry one even if you are not expecting your period – you might be able to help a fellow swimmer out. It could feature doggy bags, hand sanitiser, tissues, towelling squares that can be dampened and used as wipes, tampons, reusable pads, spare pants, paracetamol and ibuprofen and an emergency Snickers. An extra bottle of water for rinsing cloths, hands and menstrual cups is also a good idea.

367. Unless you are one of the rare people who have mastered the art of using a Shewee, going to the toilet outdoors involves baring your bum and avoiding stinging nettles. Throw in your period and it can get messy and uncomfortable. I like the comfort of a lightweight poncho for changing, and this comes in handy for a bit of modesty when changing a pad or tampon. The outdoors is for everyone, and I try to be discreet with toileting, respectful not just of my environment but other users and those who live and work in wilder places.

368. Periods are part of life and just because there are ways to deal with them when you are outdoors, it doesn't mean you have to. Listen to your body and what it needs. Some days will be a swim day, other days will be a duvet day, and that's okay. The water will still be there.

PREGNANCY* (369–378)

369. When you are pregnant your body is doing something truly amazing: you are growing a whole new human being. This miraculous process can be wonderful, but can also push you both mentally and physically to your limits and beyond. Listed here are some practical ideas to consider when thinking about outdoor swimming when pregnant.

370. It must be remembered that any advice about outdoor swimming when pregnant must be considered alongside medical advice. Many women have trouble-free pregnancies, but it would be advisable to check with your care team that there is no pressing reason why you should not swim. There is a growing understanding of the benefits of outdoor swimming while pregnant, and so medical professionals should be able to offer guidance that is tailored to each individual woman.

371. Women who choose to swim outdoors during their pregnancy need to be aware of certain key risks and biological facts. The first thing to be aware of is that, just like everyone else, each swim is different and should be risk assessed on the day. You should consider how much sleep you have had, if you have eaten well that day, your level of well-being and general health. Swimmers should never take a swim distance, temperature or location for granted. Even our local spots can become fast moving and unpredictable, temperatures can drop suddenly and all of these things can adversely affect the outdoor swimmer, including women who are pregnant. Taking care of your general well-being and cautiously approaching each swim will always pay off – as others have said, if the swim doesn't look or feel right to you, then don't go in. There will always be another day when you can get into the water.

372. Some outdoor swimmers choose to solo dip or swim. Consider always having a buddy with you if you are pregnant. From a safety point of view, having someone else there to help you if you get into difficulty is really important. Technology can also be your friend here: make sure that one of you has a mobile phone which is charged, check the signal in the area that you are going to and let people know where you are swimming. Ensure you're able to give your location via a grid reference so that if you do need to call for help people can find you easily. Another excellent reason for taking a friend swimming with you is that it can be really, *really* difficult to get neoprene booties off your feet when you are also negotiating a bump! Friends can also provide peace of mind with their company.

* Thank you to Rachel Whitfield, wild swimmer, Mental Health Swims host and photographer, for contributing this section.

Always take a buddy with you when pregnant (even if only to get them to take photos of you).

373. While we are on practical issues, we should of course consider your warm-up routine – recovery from the chilling effects of cold water is particularly important when pregnant. You will have a higher cardiac output, meaning you have an increased heart rate and a lower blood pressure and so will have a lower tolerance for exercise. This can affect how long you are able to stay in the water and also how long it will take you to rewarm and recover. Lay your clothes and warm layers out in the right order for getting dressed before your swim; consider shoes that are easy to put on instead of anything with laces; wrap your clothes around a hot water bottle for a toasty welcome back to dry land.

374. Cold water can cause vasoconstriction, which may increase blood pressure. When you are pregnant you may also feel warmer, which could encourage you to stay swimming for longer than you normally would, and so keeping an eye on the time and what is a normal swim length for you is advisable. As long as you are not adversely affected by the cold water, core vessels and placental blood flow should not be affected as the baby is protected inside the amniotic sac. Leg cramps, however, are commonplace while pregnant, but good hydration and nutrition can help to avoid them. A good excuse for cake after a swim!

375. Some women find that as their baby grows they find themselves short of breath due the baby pushing up and restricting lung capacity. This can happen on dry land as well as in the water, but it is worth remembering that this shortness of breath is very different to the gasps of cold water shock. It tends to be less dramatic, but if it is a persistent issue you should speak to a medical professional. Many women find that the water eases the burden that the baby places upon their body, including reducing pressure on the respiratory system.

376. The feeling of weightlessness in the water can be a delightful experience for women during pregnancy, and the pressure released from the joints can be a remedy to pain in areas such as the knee and girdle joints. We do not fully understand why wild swimming does so much good to our mental and physical health, but knowing that it is there as an option can be very soothing.

377. Rain washes microplastics from tyres on roads down into bodies of water, and agricultural chemicals run off into rivers. In the seas there are often releases of untreated sewage, which NO ONE should swim in. Check for sewage releases or think twice about swimming after heavy rainfall. Your baby is protected in the amniotic sac, but Weil's disease (*tip 175*) can pass through the placenta and make mother and baby very poorly. There are also many pregnancy-related conditions which would make outdoor swimming inadvisable, for instance any women whose membranes are not intact or women with pre-eclampsia, as it could have serious consequences such as seizures. At the risk of sounding like a broken record: if you are at all unsure, contact your health professional.

378. Outdoor swimming is a joyful celebration of life and what our bodies can do. It can be a beautiful and moving experience to share the water with your growing baby. With the right information and precautions, outdoor swimming can be done safely and can be enjoyed throughout pregnancy until term.

MENOPAUSE* (379–391)

379. Every person's menopause journey will be different: you can become perimenopausal from your early forties, but are likely to start to notice symptoms from your early fifties, and these can last for 10 years or more. Some people will experience every single symptom and some none at all – where you fall on the spectrum may be related to genetics (have a chat with your mum), general health, race (some studies suggest that Asian and African women tend to have more intense physical symptoms, but less psychological side effects) and your own relationship with your body.

380. The menopause is a completely natural stage in life (unless surgery or illness has thrown you into early menopause) and should not hold you back from anything. Regular outdoor swimming, in my experience, has changed how I view my body and lifestyle as I've gone through this stage.

381. Hot flushes can be embarrassing and uncomfortable, especially as they always seem to come over you when you least want them to. Cooling down regularly can alleviate the discomfort – sometimes even just thinking about lying in cold water can be soothing.

382. Night sweats can be awkward if you share a bed, but why not try a cold evening dip if you have a suitable place close to home? Failing this, an all-over body rub with a cold flannel just before bedtime can help.

383. Brain fog may affect you really badly in your day-to-day interactions at work or home – I find plunging my head right under the water when I'm swimming helps to clear my mind. A daily head dunk keeps me focused.

* Thank you to Sara Barnes (@*bumblebarnes*), year-round outdoor swimmer and freelance writer, for contributing this section.

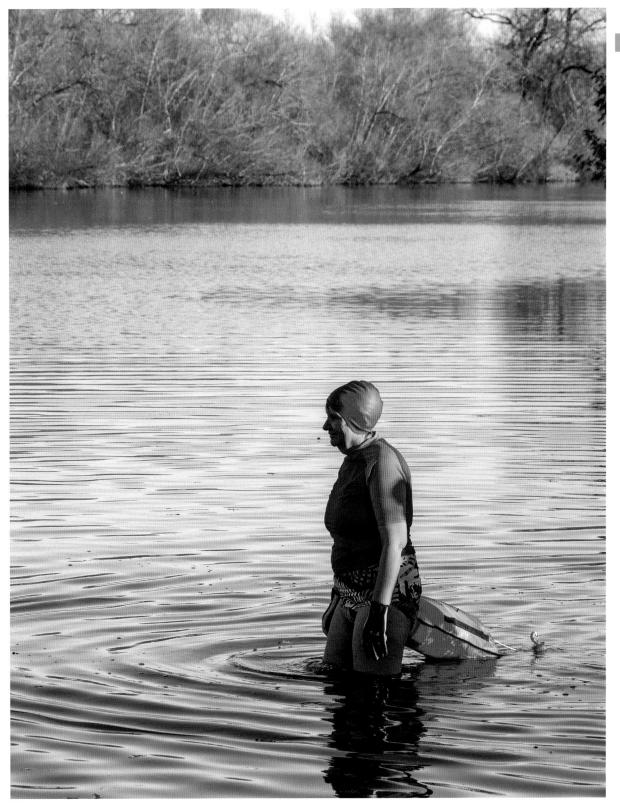

Matching your toe float to your costume is always a win. © *John Weller @wildswimminglondon*

No swimmers were harmed in the making of this photo.

384. Low mood and anxiety are one of the major signs that perimenopause has started, and these can continue into menopause. Doctors are getting better at spotting menopausal mood changes, but people are still misdiagnosed and put on antidepressants when it is our hormones once again throwing their weight around. Cold water (16 °C and under) reduces inflammation everywhere, and is considered by many to lead to significant improvement of mental and emotional side effects. The endorphin rush experienced after a swim (especially in really cold water or even ice) can last for several hours and is one of the most powerful reasons to keep dipping regularly.

385. Loss of libido at any stage in life is distressing: it can cause loss of confidence and puts a strain on a relationship. The causes can be physical or emotional, but during the menopause it is most likely down to an imbalance of oestrogen, progesterone and testosterone. Swimming in cold water improves blood circulation to all areas of the body, so everything feels more alive and active. And if you feel good about yourself, the rest will hopefully follow …

386. Painful sex goes hand in hand with loss of libido, but whether it is because the skin in our intimate areas naturally becomes thinner and more prone to damage and irritation or because our internal organs are heading south, regular swimming is a highly effective form of exercise for your body, including these areas. Top tip – try doing a set of pelvic floor exercises just as you're walking or sinking down into the water.

387. Hair loss or thinning is a natural part of growing older, but during menopause it can feel like diminishing physical beauty. Water can strip your hair of natural oils and hydration, so always use a good conditioner, avoid over-styling it and allow your hair to dry naturally.

A dip in Elter Water in the Lake District, England. © *Jumpy James*

388. Dull, dry and saggy skin is a much-hated symptom that often starts in perimenopause, and no amount of expensive eye creams and skin potions seems to help. Cold water offers a free facelift and can achieve better skin texture than many treatments can. It can also improve blood circulation and increase your metabolism, meaning skin can work more efficiently to remove dead cells and regenerate new cells. In winter it may help to use a good moisturiser on your lips and around the eyes, as these are delicate areas that suffer from exposure to wind chill, sun reflecting on the water and the cold water itself. Your feet may also require extra attention, such as sanding down and moisturising — they work hard getting you in and out of the water safely, so treat them kindly.

389. Rashes and rosacea on the body or face may appear during menopause. The temptation is to cover them with foundation or clothes, but why not allow the water to soothe any irritation and calm any inflammation? Embrace your new pigmentation.

390. An aching body and joints can be caused by natural depletion of oestrogen, which helps to maintain healthy ligaments and good levels of collagen throughout the body. Non-weight-bearing movement in the water helps to reduce any arthritic swelling or build-up of fluids in our joints: moving meditation is a great relaxant and stress reducer.

391. Aside from the physical symptoms associated with being menopausal, it is often a difficult and transitional stage of your life: it may involve ageing parents requiring more care, teenage offspring about to leave home, long marriages or relationships requiring extra work or even failing, being overlooked or sidelined at work, losing physical flexibility and energy, gaining weight and reducing working hours or even retiring early. No wonder the thought of strutting down a jetty in a small piece of Lycra might be a terrifying prospect! However, think of the jetty strut as a symbol of redefining yourself and your attitude to life. If you are brave enough to walk into bitterly cold water and swim until that insane grin spreads across your face, then you are brave enough to wear whatever you want, dance to the music of life and feel as old as you want to feel. The water empowers you to inspire and educate younger generations and helps you to choose how to live this next stage of your life. Strut your jetty as if the world is watching!

Serious game face is required when cold-water swimming.

004

COLD-WATER SWIMMING (392–456)

'You will never feel more alive and invigorated than after a swim or immersion in cold water.'

Remember, ice swimming is an extreme sport. © *Jumpy James*

COLD-WATER SWIMMING (392–456)

COLD WATER (392–430)

392. I don't bother with a thermometer (usually). Instead, I have my own tried and tested 'Scottish water temperature chart', which you can apply to your swim. Here's how it works:

Roasting	On a beautiful summer's day (you get this a couple of times a year in Britain), when the sun's been on the water all day, it's like being in a bath. You could be in there for hours – it is beautiful. That's roasting.
Decent	This happens during summer, maybe on a nice summer's day or at the end of autumn: you see a good stretch of water, the sun's been on it and you can get in there and swim without a wetsuit. That's decent.
No bad	This is when you get in and you don't want to get back out immediately. It's basically if the water doesn't cause your feet pain. Oh, that's no bad like.
Aye, alright	Aye, alright happens when you get in the water and after you paddle about for a bit your mates on the side ask, 'What's it like?' Shivering with the cold, you say, 'Aye it's alright!' 'Aye ... alright,' comes the suspicious reply from the shore.
A wee bit chilly	Sometimes it's a wee bit chilly. This is when it's pretty sore to get in without a wetsuit on. You duck your head under, you paddle about a bit, you come up you get that horrible cold head (also known as ice cream head) – that is starting to get a bit brutal.
Cold	This is pretty self-explanatory. For me, it's when I get in the water and things are starting to get a wee bit smaller – I'm obviously talking about my hands here, which get really shrunken and shrivelled in cold water. Only my hands, though – nothing else!
Baltic	This is basically when you're breaking the ice on the edge of the water to get in. It's kind of like the hokey-cokey: you get in, out and shake it all about, and make sure everything is still intact on your body. It's brutal. Baltic can also be referred to as, 'hoora cold' and 'forget this, I'm getting out now.'

This is somewhere between 'no bad' and 'aye, alright' on the temperature scale.

COLD-WATER SWIMMING (392–456)

393. You will never feel more alive and invigorated than after a swim or immersion in cold water.

394. At what temperature is water 'cold'? If we go by Fédération Internationale de Natation (FINA) competition guidance, it may come in at anything below 20 °C – this is the temperature up to which you may be allowed to wear wetsuits in a competition. To me, 20 °C is borderline 'roasting' (*tip 392*); some people might consider anything under 18 °C to be cold. A common definition of cold water is 15 °C and below, while others may say 10 °C. In summary: one person's cold might be another person's cool, so judge for yourself whether you think the water is cold rather than relying on other people's input.

395. Once you get below 10 °C or so, even a change of 1 °C can feel much more stark than at higher temperatures.

396. Forget any glamorous pictures: the reality of cold water is that it's hard work.

397. When we enter cold water, our body wants to protect itself: to keep the core warm, blood flow to extremities and the skin slows down (peripheral vasoconstriction). This is why your skin will feel cold when you get out. As blood flows back to your extremities after a swim, you'll feel powerful and more alive than ever. This is the euphoria that keeps people coming back.

398. Despite my supposed aversion to actual thermometers (*tip 392*), they can be very useful: gathering data of how the water feels at different temperatures and when your comfort levels change can help you understand how your body deals with the cold. However, I wouldn't recommend using a thermometer reading as a hard and fast rule on how long you should swim for.

399. If you're going to measure water temperature, do it at multiple places: the shallow edge of a lake could be a lot warmer than out in the depths, but also the shallow water might be colder as it freezes more quickly. As water is a dynamic environment, with many factors affecting it, you can also find warmer patches, mainly at surface level.

400. Getting used to swimming in the cold takes time: months, even years.

401. The best time to start cold-water swimming is when the water is warm. By starting in summer and continuing to swim as temperatures drop, your body can adapt to the gradual change. As the famous quote says, 'Just keep swimming!'

402. The change of water temperatures is not always a constant, gradual change: depending on your location, the water temperature may alter significantly in a matter of days.

403. Stay dressed until you are ready to swim.

404. Swim faster to produce heat: the more you move, the more heat you make.

405. Get bigger to help deal with the cold. A larger body mass helps deal with cold, effectively by creating insulation on your body. Both muscle and fat help: muscles produce heat as they get used, and larger muscles produce more heat but also require more energy; body fat provides a layer of insulation, slowing down the cooling process as you lose body heat to the water. Think of the denizens of the ocean, such as seals – they are very strong, but with a larger layer of fat (blubber) over their muscles.

The universal look of 'it's really cold in here!' © Jumpy James

406. Know what cold water shock is. When you enter cold water, your skin starts to cool. This triggers a response in your body that makes your heart rate rise, and you may gasp for air and start to panic. This can cause a heart attack and lead to drowning. Typically, cold water shock will last just a few minutes, and the more you expose your body to the cold water the more adaptation takes place and your body's shock response reduces.

407. If you find yourself unexpectedly in cold water or suffering from cold water shock, follow the RNLI's guidance of Float to Live – lie on your back, lift your legs up and stay calm.

408. Not all cold water acclimatisation is the same. By this I mean that being comfortable in 15 °C water does not mean that you will be comfortable in 10 °C water – cold water shock may return.

409. In any cold water, getting in can be the hardest bit, both physically and mentally. It's always best to ease yourself in by wading in, allowing your body to realise what is happening.

410. Don't get into the water if you're already cold. Always get warmed up and comfortable before entering the water. A good way to get warmed up for me is to perform air squats, and even press-ups, while fully dressed. Each will get your blood flowing around the body.

411. Psychology is big part of getting into cold water. Even when you have done it hundreds of times, just the thought of forcing yourself into the cold can be daunting. I have a variety of ways to handle this, but here's some of the things I currently do to psych myself up:

- I talk to myself, sometimes quietly but mostly loudly.

- I take on the persona of a fervent religious leader, and make wild and bold assertions.

- I will be ready to fight, like a boxer entering the arena of battle. With my robe on, I am Muhammad Ali making the ring-walk. I am a gladiator. My battle, however, is not with the water: it is with myself. As I put my hat and goggles on, it is like putting on my final pieces of armour. As I enter the water, I go into the arena of war. I am ready.

412. Don't fight the water; see yourself as being part of it. As you enter the body of water, remember that *your* body is mostly water, and know that you are entering into a very natural activity.

413. Even once you have adapted to the cold, take the first 90 seconds of a swim to get used to the water. Don't immediately swim or even stray into deep water if you don't have to. Let your body feel the cold around you and focus on your breathing, especially keeping it under control. This is also a good way of gauging how your body initially feels without the distraction of swimming. After the first minute you should start to feel relaxed and your focus can start to switch to the actual swimming.

414. Keep your head warm. Some people like to dunk their head in almost immediately, but I have never been a fan of this as it instantly cools you down further and will cut short what time you can stay in the water. However, if you are well wrapped up in a swim cap and will be swimming with your head in the water, go for it.

415. If you don't intend on getting your head wet during a swim, then wearing a warm hat like a woolly or bobble hat is a great solution to keeping your head warm. Being able to keep one hat on throughout the entire changing, swimming and recovery process helps preserve your energy. Carry a spare hat for after the swim, just in case it does end up in the water.

416. Your extremities (hands, feet and head) will suffer the most in cold water, and this is what can cause the most discomfort during and after a swim. Protect them with neoprene to allow yourself to swim for longer and recover more quickly.

417. If you start to shiver in the water, get out. You should be out of the water well before you begin to shiver. Shivering is the natural process of your body trying to warm itself up by involuntary muscle movement. It is energy intensive and will often occur as part of the recovery from a cold swim, but this should happen after exiting the water when you are wrapped up warm. In the water, heat from the body is rapidly lost to the environment and shivering is a sign that your body is currently too cold.

418. Learn about your body over time. I cannot tell you exactly how your body will react to the cold, and how easy your recovery process will be. A particularly hard recovery or cold swim may initially frighten you or even others around you, especially if uncontrollable shivering kicks in. Shivering is good in that it helps your body warm up, however uncontrollable shivers may be a sign of hypothermia (*tip 158*). The trick is really to keep at it over time: keep on learning over many cold swims, which will help establish an understanding of your body and how it reacts.

419. Kick or swim harder to produce more heat, but remember you will also tire more quickly.

420. Swearing out loud a lot helps. It just does. Make them creative, don't just stick with the boring effing and jeffing. A solid 10–15 swears when getting into the water translates to a good 10–15 minute swim. That's solid science.*

421. Hollering, shrieking and heavy breathing can be used instead of swearing.

422. Swimming in cold water in a wetsuit can be easier on the body than without, but it's still not easy.

* This may not be solid science.

The CLAW! (*See tip 425.*) © Hannah Kettles

423. You, the swimmer, might not be the best judge of how you are doing. Listen to your safety team and helpers. Use people you trust, and work with them over time so that they get to know you.

424. If you start to feel euphoric and warm, it's time to get out. The feeling of euphoria is pretty common after a swim and is part of the natural high that keeps people coming back to cold water. However, it will often occur just before the recovery process, so anticipate this by getting rewarmed rather than standing around feeling like a superhuman.

425. Respect THE CLAW! If your pinky finger goes walkabout and you cannot close it beside the rest of your fingers, it could be time to get out: as your arm nerves cool, muscles contract and your fingers spread until eventually your hand cannot be closed. This finger spreading also hampers swimming technique.

426. Ignore the opinion of those people who don't know about cold water and don't know you personally. Listen to those who either understand the cold or care about and understand you — give special time to the ones who understand both.

427. For your first cold swim, try swimming with a wetsuit on. At the end of your swim, if you are feeling good and not suffering, then strip the wetsuit off and swim in your costume only. You'll get an idea of how your body handles each option and what you prefer.

428. It may take multiple swims for you to understand if you prefer swimming skins (*tip 116*) or with a wetsuit; it might be an epiphany that comes immediately.

429. Hunger, thirst, being hungover and poor sleep are all factors that will make you feel colder, or feel cold more quickly.

430. Cold water just might not be for you. You can't have missed the reams of articles on the sheer joy and exhilaration of cold-water immersion, but not everyone will enjoy it: some bodies suffer more than others.

Ice swimming doesn't always involve ice being on the water. © *John Weller @wildswimminglondon*

ICE SWIMMING (431–456)

431. Ice swimming is a very extreme activity — remember that before trying.

432. Never ice swim alone.

433. The categorisation of 'ice swimming' is often accepted as swimming in water that measures 5 °C or below.

434. There doesn't have to be ice on the water for it to be classed as ice swimming.

435. You will swim slower in ice water.

436. Have low expectations of yourself initially. Some swimmers count the strokes, not the minutes.

437. Go for your first ice swim with experienced swimmers who have done it before. Treat your first few swims as immersions, to feel the cold, rather than actual swims.

438. Don't just 'give it a go'. Plan every ice swim fully, no matter what distance or time. Always remember to factor in your recovery.

439. Fresh water cools down much faster than the sea during the year, and will reach colder temperatures. It's rare for seawater to reach 5 °C, unless you are very far north or south on the planet, where the sea can reach a temperature of approximately -1.8 °C before freezing, as salt water has a lower freezing point.

440. Bodies of fresh water, especially shallower water, are susceptible to environmental and weather-related factors which can lead to dramatic changes in temperature over a period of even a few hours. For this reason, the thickness of ice may change or entirely disappear from a lake or pond. What is classed one day as an 'ice swim' may simply be 'a swim' by the next morning.

441. The 'one minute in the water per degree Celsius of temperature' rule of thumb used by some swimmers is not wise for all: this is far too vague and does not take into account the myriad of other factors at play in cold water. Just because someone else does it, doesn't mean you should do it too.

442. Don't ice swim multiple times in a day; even going into icy water every single day can become a real toll on the body. If cold-water immersion, rather than swimming, is your aim, even a period of two minutes can get you the buzz you need.

443. The ultimate goal for some ice swimmers is an 'ice mile'. It is what it sounds like. It's not for everyone.

444. In order to complete an ice mile or a distance swim ratified by one of the organising bodies, the swim must be undertaken in a standard swimming costume, goggles and one swim hat.

445. An ice mile is something that has to be built up to over several seasons of regular swimming and conditioning. You should be swimming all year round, getting used to the way the water temperature changes with the seasons. Getting into the water regularly is crucial – several times a week is recommended. If you aren't able to swim several times a week, cold-water immersion and even cold showers can be used to help replicate the cold. You may need to try and source an old open-top freezer to sit in … !

446. For safety purposes, most ice miles now take place within a standing body of water and require the swimmer to complete laps, rather than one long-distance, point-to-point swim.

447. If you're actually going to break ice, use blunt force on it. An ice axe that people use for winter walking or climbing is designed to grab or hold ice, so use a hammer or sledgehammer. An axe can be used if you have experience of using one.

448. Ice sprays everywhere when struck. Protect your eyes and know that whatever you're wearing could get wet.

449. Stay warm while you make a channel in the ice. If it involves wading, consider wearing a wetsuit or even a drysuit while making it.

450. Ice is sharp; skin is soft. Thick ice can cut you, so use gloves to move slabs around. Once you break ice, use something to clear it away from the channel or hole, such as a lightweight snow shovel.

451. Sharp ice can also cut swimming-specific wetsuits.

452. To make an ice hole in thicker ice, you can use a sledgehammer, ice-drill, ice saw or a large axe. By cutting a square, you create a small floating island of ice – this can either be lifted out from the hole or pushed down and along, so that it slides away and will sit under the ice, away from your hole.

453. Ice thickness can change overnight. Make a new assessment each time.

454. Don't walk on ice unless you are sure it's thick enough. Stay close to the sides of the body of water.

455. Never walk over ice on deep water, unless you are absolutely sure of its integrity. As I watched Finns skip straight across a shortcut of the frozen Töölö Bay in Helsinki, I was quite happy to take the longer walk around it.

456. Snorkelling in ice-cold water is a grim experience, and dangerous. I do not recommend it.

Use blunt force if trying to break ice.

Front crawl is generally the fastest and most efficient stroke.

005

TECHNIQUE AND LONGER SWIMS (457–615)

'Consistency is better than sparks of excellence. Just keep swimming.'

Head-up breaststroke allows you to take in the scenery. © *John Weller @wildswimminglondon*

STROKE AND MORE (457–486)

457. The ideal swim stroke is smooth and efficient.

458. Not all strokes will look quite the same. The tips given here are general and are designed to be somewhat applicable to most swimmers, but everyone is different. Each body has individual and unique attributes to which you can tailor your stroke.

459. Try and learn each of the four main strokes (front crawl, breaststroke, backstroke and butterfly) so that you can use each if needed. Although many long-distance swimmers will use front crawl, having the ability to switch to backstroke allows you to relieve your shoulders and neck. Breaststroke can help you get a better view of your surroundings and vary your pace and butterfly looks very cool – you're sure to impress any onlookers if you can finish your swim strongly with a good 30–40 metres of it. This also allows you to switch strokes in changing conditions, such as waves or moving water.

460. Most distance and competitive swimmers will use the front crawl, which is generally speaking the fastest and most efficient stroke, but it may be that breaststroke – either immersing yourself or with your head up above water – suits you better. The first ever English Channel swimmer, Captain Matthew Webb, completed the challenge using breaststroke. If you're a glutton for punishment or have shoulders like boulders, you could use the highly satisfying but exhausting butterfly, or even the backstroke. All of these strokes have been used to swim the English Channel.

461. Sighting (*tips 487–503*) is much more difficult when using the backstroke. Having a support vessel or other swimmers to help guide you is the easiest way. I did invent a chest-mounted, rear-view mirror product to help with this, called the BackScope, but it hasn't taken off … yet!

462. When doing front crawl, roll your body. Imagine your body as your arm when you open a door with a round handle, spinning on a long axis – your whole body should roll fully both to the left and right, making a 'U' shape with your belly button.

463. Kick from the hip. In front crawl, think of your leg as one long lever, and the drive comes from the hip. Keep your legs relatively straight but not rigid, keeping your toes pointed but your ankle and knee relaxed.

464. In front crawl, your arm should move faster as it travels past your body. The start of the pull, however, should be initially slow, building in speed. This helps you catch the water and not tire your arms out immediately.

465. Keep a neutrally buoyant position – your head and feet should be in one line. Keeping your head down keeps your hips up – engage your core to help your balance.

466. As your body rolls, rotate your head slightly to breathe – don't lift it.

467. Exhale underwater; inhale above. Master this for the front crawl. Take the time to slow your stroke right down to get it right. Breathing out above water is a waste of time and can cause problems. Plus, it feels cool to do it right. Breathing in underwater is also pretty inefficient and can lead to further problems, such as drowning.

468. Learn bilateral breathing for the front crawl. This is the ability to breathe on both sides as you swim. Having the ability to breathe on each side is also a useful sighting tool if you are swimming alongside a shore or have a safety boat: it can allow you to keep a steady distance from the side, rather than having to sight ahead frequently. A good rhythm for bilateral breathing is a breath every three strokes.

469. Bilateral breathing is not always an option: if you are swimming in the sea, you may at times be forced into breathing on one side in order to avoid swallowing big mouthfuls of water as waves hit you.

470. If you feel a wave coming towards you as you go to breathe, just wait until the next stroke to inhale. Keep a little air in you so that you are not forced into a gasp.

471. Don't open your whole mouth in choppy water – shape your mouth away from it. You will, however, inevitably swallow water on some swims and also get slapped in the face by the waves and thrown around a bit.

472. Learn to barrel roll. This is a fun, not-often-used technique that can be used as another way to breathe. At the end of your front crawl pull, use that momentum to swing yourself on to your back – breathe as you face up and continue your next stroke as you roll back around to return to front crawl. Not recommended for long distances, it's a technique most often used by boaters in swift-water situations to pull themselves into safer water.

473. In choppy water, engage your core and focus on keeping solid technique. Raise your arm higher in the water during your recovery phase (from when your arm exits the water to when it drops back in), swinging it forward rather than skimming the water. This will help to avoid your hand being hit by waves.

474. Swim at a higher tempo in choppy water. Increase your stroke rate.

475. Practise mixing your stroke in training sessions so that it becomes second nature to do so when you're forced into it.

476. Rotate your body more to help you breathe in wild conditions. Breathe more frequently and faster than in calm waters.

477. Don't worry if you miss a stroke because of a wave: stay calm and keep moving.

478. Change your stroke as you move from wetsuit to swimming skins (*tip 116*). When swimming without a wetsuit in cold water, you'll probably have to increase your stroke rate to stay warm. The increased buoyancy of the wetsuit also means you can effectively glide along the top of the water, so without one it will require more effort to stay in the same position.

479. Use your legs sparingly. A powerful kicking motion can help when sprinting, but as kicking during front crawl is a comparatively inefficient method of propulsion and uses large muscles that place a high demand on oxygen, it needs to be used sparingly over long distances.

480. If you prefer not to have your face in the water, backstroke may suit you. It also reduces the need to synchronise breathing with stroke, as you can breathe in a relaxed, regular fashion.

481. Trying backstroke in choppy water and waves may lead to the water covering your face, and this might make it necessary to switch to a different stroke.

482. The key to backstroke is keeping a good body position: keep your body tight and high in the water. Focus on keeping your hips and feet high, and if they sink gently kick them for buoyancy.

If you're a glutton for punishment, try out the butterfly stroke. © *Jumpy James*

483. Although breaststroke might be viewed as an 'easier' stroke by some, remember that some of the muscles worked are different to those used in front crawl, and that fatigue will also come into play over long distances.

484. Develop a strong kick for breaststroke; the legs provide the power of this stroke. Starting with legs straight behind you, draw your heels towards your buttocks before turning your feet outwards and pushing back with a whip-like action.

485. Many winter swimmers will employ the 'heads-up' breaststroke – swimming breaststroke while keeping your head out of the water – as opposed to standard breast-stroke, which will see you fully submerge. This helps keep your head dry so that it stays warm, which is vital in winter swimming and also allows you to take in more of your surroundings, both visually and aurally. This is the best stroke for sighting (*tips 487–503*) as your head is constantly above water.

486. When breathing during breaststroke, try not to raise your head fully vertically from the water unless you need that height to sight. Keep your face roughly pointing towards the water, in the same line as your body. You should still be able to sight by looking up with your eyes, not your head.

SIGHTING (487–503)

487. A vital skill when swimming front crawl outdoors is being able to sight. Sighting is when you look up while swimming to see where you're going. This helps you swim in a straight line and take in your surroundings as well as alerting you to any hazards or upcoming obstacles.

488. Don't look directly down as you swim (there will be no black line at the bottom of the water as there is in a pool) but slightly forward – all the while keeping your head down.

489. You can also sight to the side if you're swimming alongside a shore or object, however this should also be supplemented by sighting ahead.

490. Choose something to sight off – ideally something that sits clear of the water surface and stands out against the background. Something very obvious like a white house, a large tree or a prominent rock would work.

491. If you're sighting off a buoy or boat, choose one that won't move.

492. In some situations, using two lined-up markers can also be useful. If the back marker starts to the left of your main, forward marker but then appears on the right as you progress, your swim line has altered. A tactic like this is useful if, for example, you want to avoid sections of shallower water. For instance, if you are trying to stay in the middle of a channel which has shallow, sloping shores to each side, having two lined-up markers can help you stay centred on your ideal swimming line. Imagine flying up to get a bird's eye view of your swim, then draw an imaginary straight line from you to the back marker, through the front marker. The idea is then to swim on that imaginary line. It works in the same way that some anchorages require boats to line up buoys or poles in order to avoid submerged hazards.

493. Communicate the marker clearly to any other swim-mers, for example, 'It's the big white house on the left, not the big white house up the hill … '

494. Make your own marker – hang a bright bag or fluorescent vest in a tree.

495. You may need to change the marker you are using as a swim progresses and you move along.

Charging in is often the best way to quell any pre-swim nerves. © *Jumpy James*

496. If you lose your marker, stop and take a good look. In wild conditions you might be forced into this. Tread water or switch to breaststroke, find your reference marker and get back to your swimming.

497. Techniques for sighting vary – the most efficient is to use 'crocodile eyes' (see opposite): your eyes should break above the surface of the water, with your mouth staying in. As you reach the front of your stroke and push down at the water with your lead arm, lift your head to get your eyes clear of the water and then continue with your natural stroke, breathing to the side.

498. Alternatively, you can lift your whole head clear of the water, using that time to sight and breathe together.

499. Be aware that lifting your head fully clear of the water during front crawl can cause your hips to drop in the water, which can slow you down and break your rhythm.

500. You will have to alter your technique and sight more regularly in choppier waters. Depending on conditions I sight between every 3–10 strokes. Lift your head higher, and time your sighting with the swell.

501. No matter which style you use, the key is to try not to break your stroke. So even if you didn't immediately catch sight of your marker, continue to swim and sight again.

502. The ability to sight efficiently can also reduce wetsuit rash on the neck.

503. Don't follow other swimmers in a race or event – sight for yourself and trust your own line.

The different steps of sighting.

COACHING AND GROUPS
(504–523)

504. The best way to start swimming outdoors can be to meet others who already do via a club or group, or get professional tuition depending on your own ability and circumstances.

505. Ask an experienced swimming friend – they're often very happy to share knowledge or introduce you to swimming.

506. To find a swim group, ask around. There are more swimmers than you realise. Go to your local body of water and hang about – look for the folk with large robes, baggy clothing and big smiles.

507. There's a difference between official clubs and more informal groups.

508. Groups will usually meet informally, with everyone taking responsibility for themselves and no water safety cover. They won't charge fees, have official membership or even have a particular organisational structure or hierarchy: it's usually a group of friends who have come together via a love of swimming.

509. Clubs have an official organisation and may have more organised training sessions and events. They have an official member-ship system that could require you to follow their procedures for organised swims.

510. Surround yourself with positive people. In my experience, most swimmers are positive, welcoming and often have a rebellious streak. Negative people can sap your energy and bring in doubts.

511. One of the largest organisations is the Outdoor Swimming Society (OSS), which has done so much to push forward knowledge, gain access and share the joy of outdoor swimming. It's through the OSS that I have met many incredible people and been inspired to pursue an interest in swimming and encourage others to do so.

512. The OSS has an extensive list of swim groups on their website.

513. Many groups are to be found through social media – Facebook is a favourite. They are usually based around a locality such as a town, beach, body of water or wider geographical region.

514. Not all groups want hundreds of new members. It might be that a swim group started as a niche interest among friends, and they are just looking to keep it small. You have to respect that and not force yourself into it.

515. There's been a large increase in recent years of people offering outdoor swimming experiences, coaching and guiding of all sorts. Get in touch and make sure what's on offer is what you are looking for.

516. Consider what you want: is it guiding or coaching? They are quite different things: not all guides are coaches and vice versa. Coaches will focus on improving your swimming ability and knowledge and can help you train towards a specific goal. This can take the form of group coaching or a more personalised, individual style. Guides, on the other hand, focus on providing you with an experience that matches your expectations. This can be especially useful when visiting a new location or when you want to seek out a certain swim without lots of organisational considerations.

517. Enquire about the experience and qualifications of guides and coaches.

518. Ask around and get recommendations from other swimmers.

If you're participating in a race, accept that it will be crowded at the start. © Jumpy James

519. Some coaches or guides will set up regular, paid group swims. You may see people swimming for free in the same places at the same time. You are often paying for the safety cover provided or coaching and guidance.

520. There's a variety of groups offering different qualifications and safety courses, such as the Swimming Teachers Association, Swim England, the Royal Life Saving Society, Surf Life Saving GB and the RNLI.

521. Get yourself qualified. Even if you don't plan to use it, the knowledge gained can transform your outlook and experience of swimming.

522. Take online courses. Many organisations are now offering expert online courses on tides, winter swimming, water safety and more. Many courses are also classed as Continuing Professional Development courses (CPD).

523. Learn first aid. Take an outdoor-environment-specific first aid course such as an emergency outdoor first aid course. While usually not swimming focused, a lot of the knowledge acquired is transferable and can be applied to situations you might find yourself in.

EVENTS (524–532)

524. Why do an event? There are a whole host of reasons, from experiencing a unique swim, challenging yourself and racing others to visiting somewhere new, the social aspect and having someone else worry about organisation and logistics.

525. An event gives you a focus to shape your training or swimming around.

526. You'll learn a lot about yourself by doing an event that challenges you. It may well change you as a person and create a paradigm shift in the belief you have in your own capabilities, igniting a fire for further adventures.

527. Consider what you love about swimming and judge if that works with an event. If you seek solitude, it may not be for you.

528. If the experience of a location or swim is your main motivation, consider whether you actually need to attend an event to swim there. For swims across busy shipping channels or rivers where you'd struggle to swim otherwise it makes sense; for swims in enclosed bodies of water where people will be swimming (for free) anyway, you might not be so keen.

529. Are you paying to just swim loops around a buoy? There's nothing wrong with this, but it might be that you find you hate it – it's definitely not my thing!

530. Travel with your swimming. There are a number of specialist companies that offer swimming holidays to iconic locations all over the world. SwimTrek and SwimQuest are the best known, offering holidays and events across the globe. Depending on the trip, they will take care of almost everything from your arrival to departure.

531. Accept that in mass-start races, there is a period of everyone climbing over one another at the start. You may get kicked in the face, your goggles may disappear, you may well slap someone on the bum – it can be a wild melee. If you're a fast swimmer, get to the front and stay there. If you know you'll be overtaken, then hang back to get into your rhythm.

532. Enjoy the social aspect. Speak to new swimmers, hear their stories, how they got into the sport, why they do it and where they do it. I find the sheer infectious enthusiasm that other swimmers often have reminds me of why I love swimming, and why I started.

MENTAL PREPARATION FOR EVENTS (533–537)

533. Stay actively positive. You might feel as though you are tricking yourself initially. Don't talk about failure or what you'll struggle with: focus on what you will enjoy.

534. Swim with a smile. Try and joke through the rough times – they will be worth it to look back on.

535. Visualise the swim and how good it will feel to finish. Focus on that end goal.

536. Have another event planned. Aim to progress. This can help with the post-adventure slump that often comes after a challenge. Once you're done, enjoy the achievement but have something already lined up to focus on.

537. Before a new event or challenge, don't make too big a deal of it when you are asked about it: always say you'll achieve it.

TRAINING (538–566)

538. Take your time to warm up before any session. An easy 10–15 minutes of swimming to get your muscles engaged and blood flowing should do the trick. Don't worry if your initial few hundred metres of swimming feel rough or out of sync – take that time to feel the water and your body in the water.

539. Swim down at the end of a session. Spend 5–10 minutes swimming easily to help remove lactic acid from your muscles.

540. Plan your training and stretch it out.

541. Consistency is better than sparks of excellence. Just keep swimming.

542. Motivation is irrelevant: dedication is more important. Just getting the session done can be the challenge sometimes, when you can't be bothered and you have 10 reasons why you shouldn't. Everybody gets days when motivation has disappeared – dedication is what counts. Progress is made through the process of small improvements over time.

543. Like any sport, recovery, rest, nutrition and sleep are vital. Your fitness improves as you rest.

544. Train with others. You can push each other, keep each other accountable and share motivation and the process of training. Sometimes one training partner is all you need.

Dusk at the Applecross peninsula, Scotland.

TECHNIQUE AND LONGER SWIMS (457-615)

545. Don't turn your nose up at pool training. It may suit you better in winter. As much as I love swimming outdoors and an indoor, chlorinated pool just doesn't 'feel right', the benefits of training regularly indoors helped me hugely in becoming a stronger swimmer. This applies especially to people who suffer with the cold in winter or are in training for multisports, like a triathlon. The time and energy it takes to recover from cold water might be time and energy taken away from potential biking or running training.

546. Keep a record of your swims, either in a written diary or using an app. Even something like Strava can be useful as it will automatically log your GPS tracked swims. You don't even have to follow anyone else on Strava – have it for yourself!

547. Break up a long swim into shorter chunks. For example, instead of thinking of it as two kilometres, break it into four lots of 500 metres.

548. Count up your weekly mileage to keep track of your progress long term.

549. Swim at a time that suits you. It might be that 6 a.m. swims are your thing; it might be that you don't function until lunchtime.

550. If you miss a session, don't worry. If you miss two, don't worry.

551. Have a rest day each week. (This doesn't mean you shouldn't swim at all.)

552. If you feel rubbish, don't get down – embrace that you are learning, and we often learn the best lessons through struggle or failure. Most of your training sessions won't feel incredible – in fact, only a small number of them will. Within a training plan, the majority of your sessions might feel average, without much improvement. It takes time.

553. Keep in shape so you don't have to get in shape. This will look different to everyone, but overall I'd define it as not taking months away from exercise, unless it's enforced. Even one swim a week can help keep on top of things.

554. Supplement swim training with land-based workouts. Focus on strengthening your core. Two or three sessions a week is good.

555. Take care of your shoulders. Take the time to stretch them well between sessions. After shoulder issues, some exercises that really help me are wall slides, L-Y-W's and a variety of pec stretches. Wall slides involve sitting or standing with your buttocks and back against a wall. Place your head (in a neutral position), your shoulders, elbows and wrists against the wall, with your shoulders and elbows at 90 degrees. Keep your entire body in contact with the wall, slowly sliding your arms upward. Using slow, controlled movements, return to the initial position, breathing normally. To do an L-Y-W, you will need to lie face down on the floor, using a folded towel to support your forehead. Point your arms and shoulders ahead and raise them off the floor (if you were standing your hands would be high above your head). Starting with your arms straight overhead (this is the 'L' position), move them wide to create the 'Y' position, then pull your elbows towards your hips, squeezing your shoulder blades together, creating the 'W' position. Your hands will be in line with your shoulders. Return to the 'L' position once again. Focus on keeping the movements slow and controlled, along with your breathing. I like to repeat each exercise for 10 repetitions, and three sets of each. With all exercises, work within your body's capabilities, progressing over time.

Making friends in Oman.

556. Build your aerobic base. To swim for a long time, first get used to swimming at an easy effort. You shouldn't get out of breath or have your muscles feeling 'pumped'.

557. Work out your critical swim speed (CSS). (This isn't the pace you can do while having a moan.) CSS is the theoretical fastest pace you can hold without exhaustion, worked out over 400-metre and 200-metre time trials. A GPS watch can calculate this, and there are handy online calculators.

558. Train using interval sessions. Base these on your CSS. Start with one session a week and build up. These will elevate your heart rate and can be made more intense over time.

559. A first interval session might be three lengths of 200 metres, resting in between each repeat. Within a month you should be trying three lengths of 300 metres.

560. Put some technique-based sessions into your plan. Bad habits can creep in on long swims, especially when focus disappears and if stress or panic sets in.

561. Get your stroke analysed by an expert. It's best to get a solid, efficient technique early on: it could save you from injury woe, it's almost sure to cut your times down and, most importantly, it will help you enjoy swimming – you will feel different in the water.

562. Film yourself swimming to get a laugh at how awful your technique really is. After laughing, identify what you can improve on. This is when comparison with people who have good form can really help. Remember, however, that everyone has quirks and differences within their swim stroke – we are not robots.

563. Get a coach if you're taking on a big, new challenge; someone who can plan your training, track your progress and help guide your progress.

564. You don't need to swim the full event distance in a training session.

565. Don't compare yourself to others. Focus on your own work and improving yourself rather than worrying what others are up to. Having said that, seeing what other swimmers are doing and are capable of can be a big motivator for some.

566. Celebrate small wins and improvements.

Try to remove your cap and goggles on the move to save time in swimruns.   © *Jumpy James*

SWIMRUN (567–585)

567. Why just swim or run when you can combine the two? It's a brilliantly easy way to open up new adventures. The sport and competition side of swimrun is growing fast, but it's also a fantastic way of journeying, without the need to 'race'.

568. Run with everything you need to swim and swim with everything you need to run. To me, a journey is always far more exciting than swimming or running loops. Swimrun events are growing, but remember you can always just do your own one.

569. Most swimrun events will have mandatory kit list like a compass, whistle and pressure bandages.

570. The swimrun wetsuit. You can get specific suits for swimrun: they have a front zip (which allows you to cool down on runs), inside pockets for snacks and an outside pocket for a GPS tracker or other stuff and are usually cut off at the knees. The front zip also means you can stuff your goggles and cap inside it when you run. Alternatively, you could just cut an older wetsuit off at the knees.

571. Swim in your shoes – they will drag but it's much easier and faster than constantly taking them on and off. Use shoes that will endure training well and have good grip for the terrain.

572. If you're taking a tow float, make it a backpack one, or create a shoulder strap for a normal float.

573. Hand paddles – many racers will use them and they are legal for swimrun races, but you must practise and build up the strength to use one. If you just go for it, you risk injuries.

574. Keep your cap and goggles on for short runs (around 10 minutes).

575. Running hard in a wetsuit is brutally warm. Running easy in a wetsuit is also a sweat-fest. For longer or uphill sections, strip the suit down to the waist.

576. Drink more water than you would if only running or swimming.

577. Drop food ahead. If you can access your planned route and you're not taking part in an event or race, leave a small drop bag hidden somewhere with snacks and a drink.

578. Carry a collapsible cup or bottle if your route includes a safe water source to drink from.

579. Use neoprene calf guards or a pull buoy to help elevate your legs. Make two holes through the buoy and use elastic (bungee laces work well) to make a strap that allows the float to sit on your outer thigh during runs.

580. Don't kick too much during the swim – save your legs for the runs.

581. Kick towards the end of a swim to wake up your legs. Within the last 50–100 metres I always make sure to kick hard and get my legs ready to bear weight and run.

582. Practise transitions. If you've done a triathlon you'll know the importance of this: the faff when getting in and out of the water can add a lot of time. Try to unzip your suit and remove your cap, goggles and paddles all on the move.

583. Test your gear. Make sure you've used it and understand it before heading on any wild adventures.

584. Get a fast swim partner and use them. Many races are done as a pair, and you have to stay close. If one swimmer is faster, then tuck in behind them. Attach a long, thin elastic cord around the lead swimmer's waist, with a length to the partner, like a weird umbilical cord. Then loop the cord around them – it should sit just under their arms. Have a small carabiner attachment so it can be removed for runs. The following swimmer can stay in the first swimmer's wake and cruise. This also removes the need for the weaker swimmer to sight as much – they can put their nose on the cord and just swim.

585. Practise with your partner and know what to expect from them during a race. It's not nice seeing friends fall out halfway round a course.

ADVENTURE AND SWIM-PACKING/ SWIM-CAMPING (586–603)

586. In swim-packing or swim-camping, day-long, overnight or even multi-day trips can incorporate swimming: think backpacking but the method of travel is swimming.

587. I use a very large waterproof backpack, designed for rafting. There are also inflatable products that allow you to float your rucksack and tow it behind you. The benefit of using a backpack is that I can immediately put it on once I stop swimming – ideal for journeys involving multiple portages. I use a Watershed Westwater Backpack which, with a 65-litre capacity, has ample space for several days' worth of kit. While it's a brilliant bag, the design is not the most stream-lined for water as it is quite wide. Look for a long, narrow, tube-shaped backpack.

588. A 30–40-litre bag is usually sufficient for day-long exploration. The most important items to carry are sustenance, navigation and communication gear (such as a phone or map) and anything that will be needed to keep you warm and dry in case of an emergency (*tip 602*).

589. Make sure to float a rucksack with the shoulder straps facing towards the sky – this will help reduce drag.

590. Double bag everything. In addition to your main bag, all items should be within smaller dry bags. As well as keeping stuff dry it's also much easier to organise your gear in this manner, grouping together items of similar usage such as spare clothing in one bag, cooking gear in another, sleeping bag in another. Keep anything that's not needed during the day at the bottom of the bag.

591. Eat plenty. Swimming and dragging a bag is calorie intensive.

592. Nail your camping set-up first. Get your kit and methods sorted on a walking trip before taking on a swim-camp.

593. Give your bag enough space behind you. With it generally being bigger and heavier than a tow float, I like to give my bag more space by using a slightly longer leash. It's not much fun when you stop to look around and it ploughs into the back of your head like a big orange freight ship.

594. If you are towing multiple bags, arrange them so that they tow in a line, one behind the other. Having the bag with the largest mass directly behind you allows smaller bags to sit in the slipstream. I've swum with three in a row behind me, like a wetsuited mother duck and her ducklings.

Make sure to give your bag enough space behind you. © *Hannah Kettles*

595. You can also use products such as the RuckRaft®, a large raft on which your rucksack sits, inside a waterproof bag. Towing a packraft, other inflatable boats or even a SUP or surfboard is another option, but these aren't nearly as transportable if you're doing a journey of more than one swim.

596. Use fins – they make the journey a lot faster and easier. This will also mean needing a longer leash or line behind you. I like to leave a gap of around a metre from fins to bag.

597. Keep snacks handy. Have a small bumbag or mesh sack attached to your main bag to stop and eat as you swim. Keep paracord (a lightweight nylon rope) handy to tie extra bits and pieces to the bag. Plan your route to visit cafes and shops if you need.

598. If it's cold, take a flask. Instead of stopping to heat water up on a stove during the day, boil water in the morning and keep it in the flask, or for a more relaxing time take the chance to boil water each meal – a hot drink always raises spirits. However, if you're swimming in warm water and environments where getting cold won't be an issue, scrap the flask – it's just taking up space.

599. Leave no trace that you were there. Take only photos and rubbish.

600. Carry a first aid kit and know how to use it. Keep it in an obvious bag marked 'first aid' and keep it easily accessible. It should include surgical gloves, scissors, gauze, safety pins, compression bandage, antiseptic wipes, duct tape, plasters, a roll of micropore tape, triangular bandages, painkillers (paracetamol, ibuprofen), tweezers, a face shield and a wound dressing. Buying a pre-packed camping first aid kit is okay, but they never have exactly what you need and the quality can vary wildly. It's better to buy each item individually if you can and build up your own kit.

601. Wrap duct tape around your water bottle to make a makeshift holder and keep it handy for using.

602. Carry an emergency shelter/bothy bag to allow for somewhere to sit quickly out of the cold. They are usually a bright colour like red or orange, so can be used to get attention and make yourself visible if help is required.

603. Carrying a backpack on top of a swim wetsuit is a sure-fire way to wear out the shoulders quickly. It's okay for short walks, but on longer ones consider stripping to the waist with a different top on or padding under the shoulder straps with something soft to protect the vulnerable swim wetsuit. Even a spare T-shirt or thin towel can work. The same applies to wetsuit hips – the backpack hip straps may wear through them.

THE THOUGHTS OF THE OUTDOOR SWIMMER (604–615)

604. Don't be afraid to talk to yourself – it can help you understand yourself. I talk to myself both within my own head and out loud (usually when I am alone). Among the many topics that wash into my mind come a few that rise and stay with me, while some fall away. The following tips are some of the mantras or thoughts that flow into my mind which may help you as well.

> **605.** *You never regret a swim.* Every swim, whether the experience brings a warm feeling when you recall it or a sense of foreboding at situations you would not repeat, teaches you something and ultimately makes you a more well-rounded swimmer.

606. *It's so cold. I regret this swim.* Know what your limits are, and if you start to feel uncomfortable or in danger, get out. Uncomfortable or difficult situations often provide the best opportunities to learn from, once looked at in hindsight.

607. *It's all good training.* From the lugging of extra gear to the waterside to the forgetting your neoprene socks, or anything that requires effort and is a bit harder than you expected – it's just good training.

608. *One, two, breathe. One, two, breathe.* Keep track of your breathing, especially in cold water – it can be easy to fixate on swimming and suddenly find yourself out of breath. Establishing a rhythm can keep both your stroke and breathing in time, leading to relaxation and the calm, zen-like state induced by endurance events.

609. I often run mathematic calculations to pass the time: *So I've covered 1,200 metres so far. Now, if one yard is slightly less than one metre (0.9144 metres), how many laps of Glasgow's Western Baths (90 feet) have I done? Well, it's three feet to a yard …* By the time you've worked this out, you've probably added a few hundred metres to your distance – no, wait, a few hundred yards!

610. One tactic you can use is to imagine yourself in the computer game *Street Fighter*. Your health bar is full. Once you're in and swimming it's going down. If you've swum 20 per cent, do you feel 20 per cent tired? No? Well, you're ahead of the game! Keep a tab on that effort/tiredness bar going down.

611. The previous tip works for multiple swims. For example, if I've been in swimming and I've not fully recovered for swim two, then my health bar starts from a lower point. It recharges during rest and feeding.

612. Break down the remaining swim into percentages. If you've got 2,000 metres to go from a total of 3,000 metres, you've done 33 per cent. Do you feel 33 per cent wrecked? No? Let's go then!

613. Sometimes, it's good to think of nothing. The swim becomes a practice of mindfulness.

> **614.** I sing. A favourite is Bing Crosby and The Andrews Sisters's *Ac-Cent-Tchu-Ate the Positive.* Slowed down a little, it has a decent beat for front crawl.

615. It also helps to think about what to eat first. My thought process usually goes something like this: Pizza. Chips. Curry. Macaroni. Pizza and chips! Pizza, chips and macaroni! Curry and chips! Curry pizza … ? Hmmm …

Channel your inner *Street Fighter* (*tip 610*).

The Schlachtensee in Berlin, Germany. © *Hannah Kettles*

006

SWIMMING ENVIRONMENTS (616–775)

'That thing that just grabbed at your leg is more likely to be seaweed than a monster – but you can never be 100 per cent sure ...'

Swim venues are great places to get your outdoor swimming fix and meet other swimmers. © *John Weller @wildswimminglondon*

SWIMMING ENVIRONMENTS (616-775)

WHERE CAN I SWIM? (616-627)

616. Research your location before going. Ask other swimmers and consult the various online guides and books that exist for this purpose.

617. Try and access water at points already used by others: increased footfall can lead to damage on vulnerable terrain such as dunes or riverbanks.

618. If you're travelling by car, always park in a suitable place. Don't block driveways, gates or roads.

619. If you can, go by public transport or bike. In small, rural places parking can sometimes be a nightmare, so taking a bike either all the way or parking elsewhere and cycling to your destination is much easier at times.

620. Come to Scotland if it's freedom you seek! The Scottish Outdoor Access Code (SOAC) enshrines in law the right of responsible access, which extends to inland waters as well as land. In short, you can walk or swim anywhere you like as long as you do so responsibly. This means creating no damage, not interfering with those who live and work wherever you're going and closing any gates you open behind you. Leave No Trace.

621. You may often see the right of responsible access called the Right to Roam – this is not the same thing. Although you can access any land under the right of responsible access, you have responsibilities and must look after the land. The SOAC applies to privately owned land as well as public, so you can go almost anywhere you like. Private gardens close to houses and things like Ministry of Defence land, playing fields and golf courses are out of bounds. Don't take the mick – this doesn't include swimming in garden ponds. Some lochs have been built specifically for fishing or other uses.

622. The access is only for non-motorised transport, so activities like walking, cycling, canoeing and kayaking are included. You cannot just drive a car, 4x4 or campervan where you like. This includes camping with a vehicle – you should get permission before driving off-road.

623. There are by-laws against swimming in canals in some places, such as the UK, unless through organised, authorised events. This does not extend to the natural open water sections of the canal system, such as Loch Ness in Scotland.

624. In England and Wales ... well, it's a lot more complicated. You cannot just pick up a map and go wherever you like. Access to land and water is much more restricted in Northern Ireland, where the number of public rights of way is tiny in comparison to the rest of Britain.

625. You have a right to swim in tidal waters and waters that are navigable by boat in England and Wales.

626. Swimming in the sea is allowed in England and Wales, but getting access to it can be an issue. In some places access to the water is tolerated and welcomed, but it's not always the case. Be sure to check permissions where you intend to swim.

627. Join the campaigns. Why can't more of the UK have the same or similar rights to Scotland? Support the various campaigns to extend access, including the Clear Access, Clear Waters campaign, Right to Roam campaign and Outdoor Swimming Society Inland Access Group.

RIVERS (628–662)

628. Not all rivers are the same, and even within their courses, rivers are not uniform in their depth, current, features and water quality.

629. Plan your entry and exit points prior to the swim.

630. Experience Olympic-speed swimming by swimming in a river – in the Hurly Burly event I swam at twice the speed I would usually, and that was upstream on the incoming tide!

631. Check the river levels before you go. Environmental agencies track this data, with live information for many points along a river. This information will often tell you how high the river level is, and the relation of that to the normal range of the river.

632. Consider the river – the whole river. Although water levels may be low where you are planning to swim, rivers can rise into spate at an alarming speed during or after heavy rain. Look at the wider topography: if your river has many tributaries upstream, a large catchment area or steep ground surrounding it, it may be prone to huge increases in flow. The same applies for areas with very dry ground, either permanently dry or as a result of drought: the surrounding ground may not soak up water, so it may rush quickly into the river. I have seen a river rise from a gentle trickle to a torrent within a matter of minutes.

633. When describing a river, we use the terms river left and river right. This is always seen from the perspective of someone facing downstream, river left being the bank on your left-hand side, and river right on the right. Most experienced water users should know this – make sure whoever you are swimming with or speaking to understands this.

634. Generally speaking, it's the higher reaches of a river, where the surrounding ground is steeper and rockier, that flash floods are more likely to occur. Downstream, as a river reaches the sea, it's usually flatter and wider.

635. Unless you know you can swim the whole river, I'd advise using some kind of footwear. Shallow sections of river may involve wading or clambering over or around obstacles, such as fallen trees. You may even need to exit a river and then rejoin it where it's safe to do so. Wearing footwear – ideally something with closed toes to protect your feet – means you can more quickly navigate awkward terrain. Riverbeds are rarely uniform and may contain areas of gravel, rocks and sand as you travel along them. Wearing shoes also reduces the risk of cutting bare feet on rocks or sharp objects within a river. This especially applies in colder water where a sharp cut or nick might not be immediately felt on cold skin.

636. A recce on foot by walking the riverbank is hugely valuable, or alternatively a journey by watercraft if you are experienced at using one.

637. Look at the current. Can you swim faster than that?

638. Where a river flows straight, the water flow is usually fastest in the middle.

639. Where a river bends, the flow will be fastest and deepest at the outside.

Swimming upstream means you can relax on the return journey.   © John Weller @wildswimminglondon

640. What swims with the stream? Dead fish. Swimming upstream initially can make for a more interesting swim, as you can get to relax on the return.

641. The water does not all flow downstream at once – in many places you will find safe eddies or areas of flat water that you can relax in. Around some features, such as weirs and rapids, you will also find areas where the water flows back upstream for a short while, almost like some kind of natural river escalator.

642. Rivers can be fantastic places to snorkel: in bright weather, there can be a multitude of things and creatures to spot in the water. I've found myself face to face with a row of little eel faces as they hovered underneath a small waterfall.

643. Where the river flows into the sea and becomes tidal, you may find that at low tide the area becomes a muddy marsh. Check the tides before you swim.

644. Where rivers become tidal you may find very strong incoming and outgoing tides.

645. On the strongest incoming tides, on some rivers you get tidal bores, which are where the incoming tide creates a wave that surges upstream.

646. A river can be your own personal endless pool. By finding a spot that matches your swim speed, you can swim to a standstill, being held in one place by the current.

647. In shallower water, try defensive swimming: this involves lying on your back and going downstream feet first. Keep your knees bent and gently back-pedal your feet, so that you can bounce off any rocks. Your arms should be outstretched and doing an almost circular motion. Keep your head slightly up to look ahead, but avoid sitting up fully, unless you want your bum to smack off the ground. The idea is that you can see any oncoming obstacles and use your feet and hands to fend them off in order to keep your head safe. Swimming front crawl or breaststroke in shallower water means that your head will be leading your body and will potentially be the first point of contact for any rocks.

648. Dam! Find out if there any dams upstream of your chosen swim spot, and if there are, whether they are on timed releases. Energy companies should advertise water releases in advance, which is ideal for white-water paddlers but can sometimes mean a change of plan for a swimmer.

649. When on a faster-moving section of water that may be too shallow to swim in but you know to be safe, such as over soft ground, it can be possible to 'Superman' down the river: stretch your arms out overhead in a victory pose, straighten your body and whoosh down the flow. You'll have to be able to hold your breath and plan your ending before adopting the position.

650. Take great care around water features, such as waterfalls or rapids. As a rule, avoid white water as a swimmer.

651. Smaller features can become bigger problems: even small branches can snag a wetsuit or tow float, or cause injury.

652. Popular fishing rivers may have weirs hidden underwater. They are usually made of rock or concrete, but they sometimes also contain wire.

SWIMMING ENVIRONMENTS (616–775)

653. Take care around weirs. They may contain stoppers that circulate and can pin you. These currents can form at the bottom of a weir and can be very hard to escape from. Water falling over the weir rises back up, recirculating. Stoppers can also be formed within natural drops and waterfalls in rivers; higher water flow can make the stopper wave even stronger. An indication of a stopper could be litter or wood floating on it, trapped within a seemingly never-ending cycle of being just too buoyant to submerge and having no way out.

654. Give bridges and especially piers lots of space: they may be bigger underwater than above and can create dangerous stopper waves in high flow. Trees and other hazards can also accumulate around them.

655. Respect other water users and they should respect you.

656. Some areas of river won't regularly see swimmers, and swimmers can be viewed as a threat or nuisance by other water users. I understand this to arise from the fear of the new and unknown, and new water users appearing in a place that some people might think of as 'theirs' may not sit well with them. Remember that some people will just be against you – in this situation, walk away.

657. Swim on a Sunday. In Scotland, for example, salmon fishing is outlawed on a Sunday, so it can be the easiest day to swim uninterrupted and steer clear of potential conflicts.

658. Sight (*tips 487–503*) regularly on rivers. Modify your stroke to allow this, if necessary.

659. Don't kick up gravel beds. These are spawning grounds for fish and are where they lay their eggs during the winter; the eggs hatch in spring. The fish and their eggs are protected by law.

660. Keep low when walking in a river or stream environment. Stay loose in case of a slip, with your arms free and relaxed.

661. When walking up streams, look for where the rocks in the flow are clean, without algae or growth. Often placing your foot on to this clean rock, directly in the flow of the water, is the best bet for gripping, although it can initially seem daunting. The constant movement of water keeps it clear of growth, and can make for very easy walking.

662. Learn to identify and avoid giant hogweed. Once you identify it, it's very obvious. A large plant, its sap can burn the skin and leave affected areas vulnerable to UV damage for years afterwards. Common hogweed is widespread, and grows to a maximum of two metres in height; giant hogweed is similar in appearance but grows up to three or four metres in height. The leaves of the giant hogweed are very large, and much more jagged than common hogweed.

WATERFALLS (663–669)

663. Sit underneath gentle waterfalls. The rhythmic tapping on your head, like a million little drummers, is very satisfying.

664. Waterfalls are generally part of a river, so follow the river-swimming advice in **Rivers** (*tips 628–662*). Some 'waterfalls' also occur when the tide moves from a wider area through a narrower section, creating a horizontal tidal race. These are sometimes referred to in their name as 'falls', such as the Falls of Lora.

Enjoy the pitter-patter of gentle waterfalls tapping your head. Dochfour Burn, Scotland.

665. Look at the water first, see what it's doing. Is the waterfall or rapid creating pools of water that are circulating in the opposite direction to the flow? Is it holding objects, such as wood or rubbish? Recirculation and trapped flotsam may be a sign of a dangerous stopper wave (*tip 653*). The power of a waterfall can also carve interesting shapes underneath the water – it may have created caves or gullies that cannot be seen by the eye. From the outside, it's difficult to judge the depth of the pool underneath a waterfall, or if there is even a pool at all. Looking at the water from a safe distance can help you work this out. If the water is heavily aerated and very difficult to see, it might be best to avoid getting close to it.

666. Not all waterfalls behave in the same way.

667. Steer clear of waterfalls in spate.

668. You lose buoyancy in aerated water. This means that you'll go deeper if you jump into aerated water, and you'll struggle to swim as fast or stay afloat.

669. Test what the water does at the bottom of a fall by attaching an object that has neutral buoyancy, or a float, to a long line. Hold one end and throw it into the waterfall, observing what happens. You can see if the water pulls it down, traps it or recirculates it. If it disappears underwater and is held there, that may be what would happen to you.

LOCH/LAKE/TARN/LLYN/MERE (670-681)

670. Start swimming along the shoreline. The deeper you go, the colder it is.

671. Fresh water in general feels colder than the sea.

672. Be considerate to protected environments. Some lakes are nature reserves and designated sites, and are best left to the wildlife.

673. Beware calm, still water. A location might look idyllic, without a ripple of movement on the surface – this could be a clue that the body of water contains very little flow in or out. In some situations this can cause stagnant, foul conditions. I remember a swim just like this: the dark water hid a rank-smelling, muddy bottom. Every step released a grim smell and I didn't last long, hauling myself out on to a nearby pier. I had to get rinsed off with a hose before I could go in the house, like I was a mucky dog. To be fair, it was more memorable than some better swims I've had.

674. The thermocline is a layer which separates water of drastically different temperatures: a separate, warm-water layer floats above cold water. I have experienced thermoclines mostly in summer – especially where the sun heats a layer of warmer water at the surface – but they can exist year-round. Depending on the depth, you might feel this colder water with your feet or if you were to dive down. This is a great reason to ease into a body of water instead of immediately jumping into what might be a significantly colder patch.

675. Lakes may have currents, especially at their ends and in narrow channels. Where a large river enters or exits a lake there's often a pull, which is more pronounced after heavy rain. Sometimes this will exist along one whole side of a lake, on the same side as the river.

676. Some lakes may even have a 'tide'. These are not true tides in the sense of the sea, but factors such as a prevailing wind can cause large changes over a body of water, in a process known as seiching. An example of this is Lake Geneva, as well as Lake Garda, Lake Baikal and Loch Earn in Scotland, where the water moves back and forth across the loch over a period of approximately 16 hours.

Leaping into in the Alltan Dubh at Little Garve, Scotland.

677. Be aware that popular locations will have cans, snagged fishing lures and broken glass in the water – wear protection on your feet or take great care entering and exiting.

678. 'You don't know until you go' can cover a whole load of things, but sometimes you won't be able to get information on a location until you actually go and try it for yourself.

679. Swim in clear water, away from reeds. They won't pull you down, but you can become tangled in them. If you do get tangled, stay calm and gently ease yourself out: struggling just causes tiredness and panic.

680. If reeds trap you, elevate your legs and swim on your back, making wide, sideways motions with your arms.

681. Never call a loch a lake. ☺

SEA SWIMMING (682–725)

682. That thing that just grabbed at your leg is more likely to be seaweed than a monster – but you can never be 100 per cent sure … In the event of actually getting a leg tangled while swimming, relax and slow down. Gently pull your leg free, and remove the monster's tentacle.

683. Location choice is vital when swimming in the sea. Choosing somewhere that will allow you a safe swim involves thinking about a multitude of factors: tide, currents, swell, entry/exit, water quality, other users and more.

684. Swim where other people regularly swim. This can allow you to tap into local knowledge and infrastructure. Speak to local swimmers, use their experience and recommendations.

SWIMMING ENVIRONMENTS (616–775)

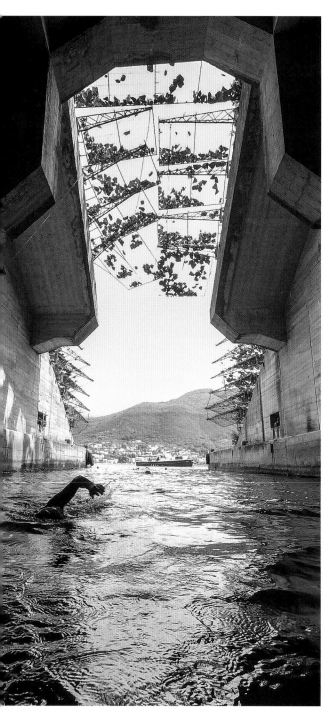

The Submarine Tunnels in Montenegro.

685. Some popular beaches are patrolled by lifeguards, who will set out a designated swimming area, often between a set of coloured flags. Follow their advice and don't take the mick: even if you are a strong swimmer, distracting them from work could leave someone more vulnerable in danger.

686. Swimming in a location that is considered dangerous by a local population could end up causing you difficulties, even if you think you are a strong swimmer. If you are alone in the water, a passer-by may think you are in trouble and alert the authorities, even if you are having a whale of a time. I've had the coastguard called for me by people who had the right intentions, but didn't know what they were looking at. Mind you, diving off my SUP and then swimming back to shore towing it behind me might not have been the wisest move, in hindsight.

687. Seawater makes you more buoyant – you may well swim faster.

688. Choppy seas can make for very messy swimming – you may well swim slower.

689. When taking on a challenging swim or crossing, making relevant bodies and organisations aware of your plans is crucial. Find out if you are swimming through any harbour areas, shipping lanes or military exercise grounds. Often a phone call to the coastguard, lifeboat and any relevant harbour authorities is a good start as they can advise you on potential hazards and even arrange a time window.

690. Your swim can have knock-on effects. When I swam across the Firth of Forth near Edinburgh, I was given a generous two-hour window to make the swim. Unfortunately, my safety boat was an hour and a half late getting to the start, meaning we then caused a huge oil tanker to have a delay. So if the UK GDP took a quick dip (wahey!) that day, now you know why …

691. The sea is not our home, but it is home to others. Sea swimming can be one of the best ways to view or interact with sea creatures, but keep it on their terms: try not to approach animals and allow them to come to you if they wish. If in doubt, it's always better to leave them be.

692. Don't touch marine life. Unless you are absolutely sure of its safety, avoid touching it. This includes some shells, such as cone shells which may appear empty but can contain the extremely venomous cone snail (not usually found in the UK).

693. When swimming in areas of great underwater flora and fauna, try to float soon after entering the water. This reduces the risk of trampling on seabed creatures, and also reduces the chance you'll hurt your feet.

694. Consider shuffling when entering the water on sandy beaches. In summer, creatures such as weever fish or stonefish will sit in sand and, when stood upon, inject a venom into the sole of your foot. This is another reason to consider beach shoes. Take great care in areas of coral, to protect both it and your skin.

695. The best cure for a weever fish injection is to immerse that body part in the hottest water you can bear, as soon as possible. The fish injects a protein into your foot, which is denatured by the hot water.

696. If the data is available, find out about sewage releases. In many countries, raw sewage is at times discharged directly into the sea. This is worse during and after heavy rainfall, and around large population centres.

697. You don't have to go into deep water. A swim along a coastline is often far more interesting than heading out into the deep just for the sake of it: you are more likely to see things of interest, it can be easier to keep your bearings and it will allow anyone on land to keep an eye on you.

698. Watch the waves before you get in. Waves come in sets, with lulls in-between. This will help you know what to expect and judge the best time to enter the water.

699. Duck dive (*tip 115*) and swim under waves. There might be no more beautiful sight than that of the curl of a wave whipping above you. It also helps you avoid the power of the waves – just be aware of the next wave when you surface.

700. Learn about tides. Generally speaking, there will be two high and two low tides in each 24-hour period.

701. The tide is controlled by the moon and can be predicted.

702. There are tide tables available for many locations, which you can buy up to a year in advance.

703. The strongest tides – or the biggest difference between low and high water – are spring tides. These occur when there is a full or new moon. Neap tides are where the tidal range is at its smallest, and occur on half moons.

704. The largest spring tides happen around the spring and autumn equinoxes.

Finding your own secret spot can be much more satisfying than following the crowds. © *Jumpy James*

705. Tides are very specific to locations. Some places have mixed tides, where different tides meet. Learn about local tides: you can't know for sure what the sea will do just by turning up and 'having a go'.

706. Often the best (and sometimes only possible) time to swim is in slack water or slack tide. This occurs around one hour either side of high or low tide, with the water being much calmer and in some places not moving at all. However, in some locations it may be safer to swim at low tide. To reiterate: tides are very specific to locations!

707. The Rule of Twelfths. This is a rule of thumb to work out the height of the tide at any given time. Split the flooding (incoming) tide and ebbing (outgoing) tides into six hours each. The tide comes in and out gently in hour one, getting faster in hour two, with the greatest flow of water in hours three and four, accounting for 50 per cent of the tide's volume. The flow slows again for hours five and six before the slack water.

708. Learn to read tide charts. Websites such as *www.magicseaweed.com* or *www.willyweather.co.uk* are invaluable and should always be consulted prior to a swim. These websites cover locations across the globe.

709. Swim on an incoming tide rather than outgoing if slack water is not an option. Depending on your location, swimming on an outgoing tide can put you at risk of being pulled out to sea. An outgoing tide may also expose rocks or dangerous terrain, such as quicksand. Even in a 'safer' location, swimming on an outgoing tide might mean you are left with a very long walk back to your bags at the end of your swim.

710. Some beaches can be swum at in any tidal height, but you need to get to know a location before you can be sure of this.

711. Some places have no tide. If you swim in the Mediterranean, you'll find the sea there barely goes in or out, it's just … there.

712. If you're unsure about currents or tides, don't risk it.

713. Learn how to spot a rip. A rip current or rip is a section of deeper, fast-moving water that moves out to sea away from the shore, almost like a river in the sea. It's what surfers will use to get pulled out to the waves quickly, but they are extremely dangerous to swimmers. They can be hard to spot, but to find one, stand on the shore and look at the waves; signs of a rip are a patch that is darker than the surrounding water, with a rippled surface and less-frequent breaking waves.

714. Not all beaches will have a rip, and the location of some rips can change.

715. Rips are at their strongest in the middle two hours of an ebbing tide.

716. If you find yourself caught in a rip unexpectedly, don't panic. Don't try and swim against the flow. Instead, remain calm and look to swim parallel to the beach, out of the current. You may find yourself pulled further out to sea, but stay calm. Once out of the rip, swim back to shore.

717. You can use a rip to get out behind breaking waves and into deeper, calmer water to swim in, but only if you are a very experienced swimmer. If there are surfers on the beach, look at where they travel out to get beyond the waves. They will use the pull of the rip to get themselves out to deeper water quickly.

718. Salt tongue? Try washing your mouth out with diluted mouthwash. This can be done during a long-distance swim. Alternatively, keep your mouth shut as much as possible. The constant action of salt water on your tongue, mouth and throat can cause inflammation and pain and in the worst circumstances make it very hard to swallow. Salt tongue or salt mouth can mean the end of your swim, if you cannot fuel correctly.

719. The ocean is salty, but some seas are saltier than others. A saltier sea means more rancid salt tongue.

720. Salty skin is harder to dress with clothes; salty, cold skin is even worse. Pulling socks on to damp, or even mostly dried salty feet can be a nightmare. If there is no fresh water around, taking a bottle of drinking water to rinse your feet is a big help.

721. If you suffer from seasickness try eating ginger (such as ginger biscuits or tea), taking non-drowsy seasickness tablets or wearing a seasickness band.

722. Avoid whirlpools. No matter how strong a swimmer you are, they can pull you under and hold you down.

723. Swimming on an incoming tide helps avoid areas of quicksand.

724. Learn about seaweed – the right stuff can make a nice little snack.

725. The sea is far more powerful than you – always respect it.

QUARRIES (726-730)

726. That lovely turquoise colour might be unhealthy. Quarries are usually the product of mining, so depending on what was mined, metals can bleed into the water. Consider what you know about the history of the quarry and what raw material was mined from it.

727. Have a look for old equipment. This can be a hazard but also an attraction, and an insight into the quarry's past life. They might have a lovely collection of old, battered cars that have been dumped in there over the years.

728. Wear footwear. Quarries are littered with sharp rocks, old bolts and pieces of wood.

729. Like reservoirs, quarries are deep and cold, often with a very pronounced thermocline (*tip 674*) and sharp shelves that drop away suddenly.

730. Some seaside quarries will contain a mixture of fresh and salt water.

RESERVOIRS (731-737)

731. A reservoir is a human-made or altered body of water created for the purpose of storing water for usage, usually as a water supply or part of a hydroelectric system. Depending on their use, they vary in size: some reservoirs might take up an entire valley while others are smaller than a football pitch. They are similar to quarries in many ways but are usually still in use; both may well have deep sides that fall away sharply. Reservoirs usually contain some form of dam, built to keep the water in. Much of a reservoir's infrastructure and machinery could be around the location of the dam, although a lot of this may be hidden underwater.

732. Not all reservoirs or all parts of every reservoir are inherently dangerous, but take caution and pay attention to any warnings at the site.

A quiet spot at Banishead Quarry near Coniston in the Lake District, England. © *Jumpy James*

733. However, there are hidden dangers. Many reservoirs will have hidden intake structures or underwater structures.

734. Some reservoirs were villages before they were flooded, and so may contain old buildings, roads and bridges.

735. As waters in reservoirs often have no or very little flow, they can be susceptible to blue-green algae (*tips 133–136*) and contain thermoclines (*tip 674*). Water movement is significantly less than in rivers and the sea, but the water in reservoirs is rarely completely still.

736. Stay away from anything human-made like dams, spillways, water intake structures, pipes and pump houses.

737. There may be a sudden change of depth.

URBAN SWIMMING (738–745)

738. You don't always need to travel to rural or remote places to enjoy swimming outdoors. Many cities have pools and designated swim areas dotted around them. While it might not be 'wild' or in a natural environment, the thrill of dooking is still the same. There are also a multitude of potential swims just waiting to be taken advantage of in our cities – just because someone doesn't yet swim there, doesn't mean you can't (as long as it's legal). Across the world many urban waterways, from rivers to canals to coastal inlets, make fantastic swims.

739. Visit Switzerland to see how the Swiss have embraced urban swimming with their rivers. It can even be a way to experience a journey through the city.

740. Take extra care when jumping in urban waterways. If you've ever seen the results of what magnet fishers (fishing for metal using a high-powered magnet) pull up, you may understand. Scooters, trolleys, poles and even weapons get dredged up from the depths.

Be prepared for adverse weather conditions. © *John Weller @wildswimminglondon*

The Mixed Pond at Hampstead Heath, England. © C. Marks – MLC Swimmers

741. Remember to take some of the same precautions as you would in a remote place. Just because you are closer to other people and help is potentially nearby, it doesn't mean you can be reckless. Cold water and its effects will be the same no matter where you are, even if the coffee shop is closer.

742. Is it legal to swim in your town or city? Well, if it isn't currently, then why not? Getting involved in local campaigns can be the catalyst for change.

743. Double-check water cleanliness. Urban waters can be liable to sewage overflows or litter being thrown in and can even be used as dumping sites by the lazy. As always, tap into the swim hivemind and ask the locals where's good.

744. Don't feel afraid of being labelled weird if you're the only one swimming – there are worse pursuits. There will be other people who would love to do the exact same and haven't yet got the knowledge, bravery or opportunity to do so. In becoming 'that person who swims', you will in time encourage others and may start a movement that can force cleaner waters.

745. Use it as a commute. If you live by a river that offers clean enough water then pack your clothes and work stuff into good dry bags (multiple bags for electronics) and float downstream towards the office. You will start work inspired and more focused than before. Bear in mind you'll never be able to say you were stuck in traffic again …

SWIM VENUES (746–751)

746. Depending on where you are, a paid swim venue may be your best, easiest or even only choice of location.

747. Swim venues are a great place to introduce new swimmers to the sport: they can develop skills and confidence in a controlled environment.

748. Somewhere with a cafe and changing rooms can be a lot more pleasant than a rocky shoreline.

749. Check before you go – some places have specified swim-only times, with slots for other sports too.

750. Bring everything you'll need for a swim. Some places will hire gear and wetsuits, but not all – check ahead. If you're hiring a wetsuit, remember that someone has probably already peed in it, even though they'd deny it.

751. Perform your own risk assessments – many of the same risks that would be at an unsupervised lake will still exist. You should still take responsibility for yourself.

SWIMMING ENVIRONMENTS (616–775)

SWIMMING TO ISLANDS (752–756)

752. Check if there's a ferry to the island you're going to. Check its timetable and route, and don't swim in the ferry's way. This may force you to plan an early swim in order to avoid boat traffic, especially in busy or popular locations. The Bay of Kotor in Montenegro offers a stunning swim to the beautiful Our Lady of the Rocks in summer, but unless you have a support boat you'll be playing dodgems with traffic during the height of the day. The solution is to embrace sunrise and get out of bed early, or wait until late afternoon.

753. Find out about the currents – some coastal island crossings may only have a short window during slack tide in which it's calm enough to swim directly over. With forward planning and common sense, these can often be dealt with.

754. Ask advice – kayakers are an excellent source of knowledge and have collectively explored almost every inch of the coast. Take their advice seriously, but remember they may not be swimmers themselves and could also be risk-averse when it comes to making recommendations to swimmers.

755. During summer some islands – both coastal and inland waters – will have restrictions on landing and time spent onshore to protect nesting birds. Some birds have legal protection.

756. Know what's on the other side of a body of water. Make sure you can get out before you start.

DISCOVERING YOUR OWN SWIMS (757–775)

757. The route to success is paved with failure. Half of the places you visit might be rubbish, but perseverance is how the gems are found.

758. Loads of my favourite finds follow this process: look at an area of the country that you're interested in; find a remote loch or river on the map; google it and find a fairly average picture or two (usually not taken by swimmers); see that it has potential but isn't widely known; go there and be amazed.

759. Use maps – either real-life paper ones or in apps. Ordnance Survey are the standard in the UK; the 1:25000 scale will give you the most detailed information. Harvey Maps also produce excellent maps, aimed mostly at hillwalkers.

760. Learn the language of the land. Understanding place names in the local language of the area you're in can open up so many ideas of a place before even seeing it. As you travel, many maps and places will be written in languages other than English, and the more of the language you pick up, the more opportunities are presented to you.

761. If you're in Scotland and want to find big fish, head to Lochan nam Breac Reamhar (Small Loch of the Fat Trout). Want to find a (supposedly) bottomless loch? Well how about Lochan gun Ghrunnd (Small Loch Without a Bottom)? How about beautiful green water? Search for Lochan or Loch Uaine (Green Loch) – there are a few of them in the hills and they are usually exactly as described.

762. One of my favourite apps is OS Maps – literally Ordnance Survey maps on your phone. You can view the maps, plot routes and switch to a satellite view to give all sorts of clues when you identify a spot.

Look at a map of the area you're visiting to find your own secret spots. © *John Weller @wildswimminglondon*

763. If a waterfall is named, it's more than likely worth a visit but may not be swimmable.

764. Waterfalls are not all named, but many will be marked by a small black line across the blue of the stream/river on OS maps. You might need to look very closely to spot some.

765. Not all waterfalls are marked on maps.

766. Pin your own favourite spots or planned visits on Google Maps – build your own collection.

767. Learn to love walking. Many of my favourite places are far away from roads – it's just a geographical fact that some amazing spots will be inaccessible to many people. But this doesn't mean that all of the best places require hours of hiking in the hills: very often this can just mean looking in less obvious places, or walking a short distance from a popular spot to find something just as good.

768. Despite my love of it, remember you don't have to go hiking – many of the best bodies of water in the UK can be driven to, or very near to.

769. For clear water, head for the hills; rocky streams are often crystal clear.

770. Find your marbles … if you can find an area with good marble deposits, you can find some of the best pools imaginable. The colour of the marble underwater, viewed from above, is quite incredible. I've never failed to be uplifted or blown away when discovering a marble-lined pool.

771. Rock pools and coastal areas can also provide amazing water clarity, but storms and big swells can sweep sand and debris into the water.

772. High mountain lochs or tarns in rocky terrain are often crystal clear, but are brutally cold all year.

773. Visit spots in multiple weathers. Drought and heavy rain can both create and destroy locations, and provide vastly different swims.

774. Visit in all seasons. Water clarity and access are sometimes only good for one season.

775. Beware who you tell. Secret spots have a way of becoming not so secret.

That post-swim joy. © John Weller @wildswimminglondon

007

GEAR (776–884)

'Don't pee in your mate's borrowed wetsuit.'

Give your gear a good check before each swim.   © *John Weller @wildswimminglondon*

GEAR (776–884)

GENERAL (776–785)

776. All the gear but no idea … you don't need it all. In fact, you don't need any of the gear: most people can swim naked.

777. There are a whole host of swimsuits available: one-piece suits, jammers, budgie smugglers, long-sleeve tops, tankinis, leggings, bikinis, burkinis, mankinis … choose the style you like best (and one that is legal where you swim).

778. Buy cheap, buy twice. Good quality gear is better value in the long run.

779. Salt water chafes more than fresh water.

780. Lubricate yourself to prevent chafing at friction points. The more you wear, the more chances of something rubbing.

781. There are a variety of lubricants available – lanolin is probably the favourite among long-distance swimmers, with Vaseline, Channel grease (a home-made mixture of lanolin and petroleum jelly) and Body Glide® also popular.

782. Don't use goose fat, you are not a roast potato.

783. Use gloves when applying lubrication, and have a rag or old towel handy to wipe your hands. It's a messy business.

784. If applying lubrication yourself, make it the last thing you do before swimming. Pack all your clothes away and have your goggles on already.

785. Lubricants won't keep you warm – the main purpose of them is to help prevent chafing, especially at rub points. Key points to cover include armpits, the neck, shoulders, between the thighs, nipples and around the edges of any swimsuit. Want to be safe? Slather it all over.

WETSUITS (786–816)

786. You may swim faster in a swim wetsuit.

787. Not everyone swims faster in a wetsuit.

788. You won't swim faster in all wetsuits – not all wetsuits are equal. There is a big difference between using a 'steamer' (full-body neoprene) surfing suit compared to a triathlon or swim-specific suit.

789. You get what you pay for, generally. A higher-end suit can help you swim a lot faster by giving you a better body position in the water, less water absorption and allowing your arms more flexibility and freedom. There will usually be more panels and features on a higher-end suit, and it'll be lighter and often easier to take off.

790. Wetsuits are a mixture of thickness, depending on the section of the suit. The panels will vary between three and five millimetres on average, with thinner sections.

791. You want a tight suit. It shouldn't be uncomfortable but should fit snugly, like a second skin. Suits can look tiny when taken out of the box for the first time – you may initially think you've been sent a size too small.

792. If your aim is to stay warm in the water rather than cover distance, use a thicker, surf-style wetsuit.

793. To keep warm, get a cold-water-specific suit. Look at wetsuits branded as 'thermal' – these suits usually have a thicker, fleece-like lining which adds hugely to their warmth; it also makes them more restrictive and thicker. Swimming in these suits can seem like harder work, but maybe it's all just good training.

Steamer, swimrun, thermal. Wetsuit designs vary according to usage.

794. In very cold conditions you may be better off using a thicker, five-to-seven-millimetre surf suit. Admittedly, this will make swimming a lot harder. You have to weigh up whether you could swim fast enough in a thinner suit to stay warm or whether you should go for the comfort, but restriction, of a thicker suit.

795. Most swimming and triathlon wetsuits are designed to help you swim front crawl. They function best when your body is in the front crawl, lying-down position. If you prefer breaststroke, look for one that is branded as 'open water' or suitable for different strokes.

796. To pee or not to pee? Cold water makes you want to wee, so it can't be avoided. I've peed many a time in wetsuits, even on dry land, and once during a conversation, staring a friend directly in the eye … I've never found it to damage the suit's integrity. Whether I've damaged my own integrity by revealing that, though, is another question …

797. Don't pee in your mate's borrowed wetsuit.

798. If you do pee, rinse your suit – during a swim if possible, but at a minimum at the end of a swim. Urine can cause a rash, and if left unwashed your suit will smell. It's a good idea to periodically wash a well-used wetsuit using a wetsuit-specific product, like Rip Curl's P*ss Off.

799. Clean your wetsuit after each swim. The easiest way to do this is simply take it off and rinse it in fresh water. I like to rinse it in the body of water I have swum in, and then again at home in a bucket or with a hose.

800. Make sure to dunk your suit well after sea swimming. Leave it to soak for several minutes in a bucket of fresh water.

801. Let your suit fully dry. Hanging it to drip and air dry is the simplest solution. Hang it inside out and folded at the waist, and use a wetsuit-specific hanger – I use a Finisterre one.

802. A great way to quickly remove moisture from a wetsuit is to lay a large, dry, absorbent towel on a flat, clean surface. Lay your suit (and other wet accessories) inside out on the towel, then roll the whole lot up, like you would with a camping mat. Lots of water will be absorbed by the towel, speeding up the drying process.

803. Don't hang your wetsuit too long, especially not by the shoulders, as this can cause weakening and damage. Hang it from the waist and, if not being used, store the suit flat and folded into three: behind the knees, then just above the waist. Make sure it's fully dry before storing.

804. Keep your suit out of the sun: UV rays will break down the material more quickly.

805. Take the time to put on a wetsuit properly. Rips will often happen around the joints, such as shoulders or hips. Pull the crotch area up fully – there shouldn't be too much excess hanging between your legs. Pull the arms of the suit on fully and get it right into your armpits. A good way to see if your suit is on properly is to stretch your arms overhead, as you would when swimming front crawl. If you find you cannot reach up as far as you would normally, it may be that the suit needs to be pulled up more. If you struggle to get your feet in, put a plastic carrier bag over your foot to slide it through.

806. Pull the suit up piece by piece – don't pull from the top. As you are getting the legs on, shuffle the suit up your calves, then thighs. What you want to do is pull small sections up at a time, rather than exert a large pull through the suit at the end.

807. If the cord to pull up the zip is too short for you, attach a further piece of string or cord – a reef knot should do the trick. Or get a friend to pull it up.

808. Wearing a wetsuit may leave you colder in the changing process if it's a real faff to get off.

809. I've found the best way to get the legs off is to almost make 'pistol fingers' with both hands: using your index and middle finger, slide both down a leg all the way past the ankle joint. This is far easier than just standing on the suit trying to hoick one leg up at a time.

810. Swimming wetsuits with a shiny outer surface are very liable to get nicked on sharp or rough surfaces. Keep your nails short or wear cotton gloves to get your suit on. Avoid sitting or shuffling on sharp rocks, and try not to walk through undergrowth or past branches or bushes.

811. Wetsuit glue will save many tears. Use a product like Black Witch to fix nicks and tears. I also like using patches for the inside of the suit, although I have found these will commonly work their way free.

The 'pistol fingers' method – see *tip 809*.

A unique swim spot in Oman.

812. Some people will tell you to get water inside your wetsuit immediately when entering the water, to allow it to warm inside the suit. This works for some suits, but in my experience not for all, and can in fact lead you to chilling sooner. Many swimming wetsuits are designed to be effectively waterproof, so that you float on the water rather than absorb it.

813. Flush water through the suit as you exit to help get it off quickly. As you get ready to rise out of the water, open the zip and pull your neck forward to allow water to come in. This will also cool you down.

814. You may get wetsuit rash/burn where the wetsuit rubs repeatedly against the skin. This often occurs on the neck, either when breathing or sighting. Good swim technique can help mitigate this (*tips 457–503*).

815. You can use a lubricant such as Body Glide® or even Vaseline on an affected area of wetsuit rash/burn. Make sure to clean these off your suit after swimming. Putting tape, or even electrical tape, on any areas you know could be affected beforehand can also work if you've not got anything else.

816. The worst wetsuit rash happens in salt water.

EARPLUGS (817–821)

817. Use earplugs. Especially in cold water or if your head is going to be in the water. Repeated exposures to cold water and wind can lead to a condition known as surfer's ear which causes a bone growth, narrowing the ear canal. The eventual solution to this is surgery that involves the bone being removed, with the ear being cut and then stitched closed.

818. Some people can feel nauseous when cold water enters the ear – earplugs can help prevent this.

819. There are a variety of styles of earplugs, from cheaper ones that resemble pieces of Blu-Tack® to custom moulds. I currently use a popular silicone design by Auritech that still allows me a reasonable level of hearing.

820. Attach a long, thin cord to your earplugs to help avoid losing them.

821. Swimmer's ear is a different condition to surfer's ear (*tip 817*), and is an infection of the outer ear canal. This painful condition is caused by water staying in the ear after a swim, creating an ideal environment for bacteria to grow. Drain your ears properly: dry your outer ear, then lean your head to the side so that the affected ear points towards the ground. Gently pull and wiggle your earlobe but avoid putting anything into your ear. If you can feel or suspect you have water inside your ear, it can take a few minutes for the liquid to trickle out, so enjoy a little lie down. Moving your jaw around or chewing, in the same way you might to help clear your ears on a plane, can also help loosen water.

TOW FLOATS (822–836)

822. A tow float or buoy is a device to improve your visibility to other water users. It is a large, brightly coloured bag or float that clips around your waist and floats behind you via a short leash.

823. Another option is a torpedo float, as used by lifeguards during rescues. Made from foam, they are designed to allow you to recover but have a much lower profile of visibility in the water.

824. A tow float is designed to make you visible in the water, but not to help you float. Tow floats should never be relied on as a life-saving device, but rather as a beacon to show others where you are.

Always be aware where your tow float is, especially when swimming with others. © John Weller @wildswimminglondon

825. Try different designs. Some tow floats double as bags, some are just basic floats and others can be used to carry snacks and drinks for longer swims, such as ones with a 'doughnut' design that allow you to access your food easily.

826. If using a bag float, put a bottle of water in it to stop the float from flailing around.

827. If you're using a phone, always double it up inside another dry bag or case.

828. A large, waterproof backpack that can be sealed closed can also be used.

829. Use your tow float as a bag on long swim journeys – they often have a capacity large enough for shoes, clothes, snacks and a phone.

830. The more stuff in your float, the heavier it is, so the more it will sit in the water rather than on top. This can cause more drag.

831. On the other hand, more drag is all good training!

832. Take extra care with tow floats when swimming in currents, or past obstacles that could snag on the bag such as branches and trees. When floating down shallow river sections with a float, I will occasionally hold it by my side/on my chest, but this can obscure your vision. You can 'otter' downstream: imagine yourself as an otter, on its back, eating food.

833. In very choppy conditions or with a tailwind, tow float leashes can get tangled in your arms or thrown forward towards your head. You can clip the float directly on to the belt, if a strap on the bag allows. It will then sit on the belt.

834. Alternatively, have the leash connected from your belly-button area. This shortens the leash behind you so it floats between your legs, but beware sitting up in the water as the leash will then yank up into your crotch!

835. Clip the belt closed when not in use. You will lose it otherwise.

836. Consider clipping free. If you find yourself in an area of reeds, branches or something that may snag the float, free yourself proactively from it.

You don't need a changing robe to swim outdoors, but it does make the changing process a lot easier.

GOGGLES (837–858)

837. There are various styles of goggles and they really are quite an individual thing, especially when it comes to fit – all faces are different.

838. My general go-to pair are Zoggs Predator Flex with a clear lens.

839. Open-water goggles are goggles that sit in the eye socket but often with a larger, more comfortable seal and larger lenses than pool or competition goggles.

840. Mask goggles are not like dive masks with nose coverings – they offer a wide-angle view and seal against the cheeks and forehead rather than directly around the eyes. Often they contain one single lens, without a nose bridge. They can help swimmers who suffer with very cold faces or 'ice cream' headaches.

841. Swedish goggles are minimalistic goggles without a rubber seal. The plastic lens sits just around the eye and takes a bit of getting used to. I've never quite mastered them myself, but some swimmers swear by them.

842. The lens you use depends on the swimming conditions. Some goggles have interchangeable lenses, but I prefer to have a few pairs handy.

843. Clear lenses are best for darker, overcast days, when light levels are low. If seeing into or under the water is also a priority for you, go for clear lenses. However, they make swimming on bright or sunny days more uncomfortable.

844. Tinted lenses can help reduce glare – a smoked or blue lens can be used in multiple different situations. You can find a variety of tints.

845. Polarised lenses are good for bright, sunny days. They cut out sunlight reflected on the surface of the water and make things appear sharper. They also split opinion into two sharply contrasting groups …

846. Although many amber/yellow tinted lenses will enhance light, some reduce brightness and so at first glance are not as good for dark days. However, I do sometimes use them to play a slight psychological trick: making it look like a sunnier day than it truly is. I'm sure there must be some maxim based upon this …

847. Mirrored lenses can help cut out glare and do look cool. But they make dark days even darker, and can hide the truth: from a safety perspective, looking into someone's eyes can help give a clearer picture of how they are, and mirrored lenses can make this hard.

848. Photochromatic lenses change their tint depending on the light conditions, so should be usable in most situations. In my experience, they can still be a bit too dark during gloomy winters.

849. Don't swim too deep with goggles on – you can't equalise pressure without a dive mask.

850. Keep your goggles in a case or soft-fibre bag – they will get scratched otherwise.

851. Carry a spare pair. Straps eventually break or come free.

852. A higher price does not always mean a better product. You can find almost any combination of strap, lens and nose bridge under the sun, often with a hefty price tag.

853. There are many bargains around. I really rate the Lomo brand for excellent value for money, but some items do sell out quickly.

854. If you use glasses you can get goggles with lenses specific to your prescription. I use the Aqua Sphere Eagle and really like them, although I usually swim with contact lenses in when wearing goggles.

855. You can get mask goggles that can fit over glasses.

856. Tie a string around the legs of your glasses.

857. Goggles will steam up – plan ahead for it. Most come with an anti-fog coating on the inside, but this will fade. There are a variety of anti-fog sprays available – I've found them pretty good, but a baby shampoo can do just as good a job. Put a few drops on the inside of the lens, fully coating it, then gently rinse the excess off in fresh water and allow the goggles to air dry.

858. Just use spit! To be honest, this is what I use 90 per cent of the time. Spit into your goggles and swirl it about until it covers the lens, rinse in fresh water and away you go. I even rinse them in seawater, as often I forget to plan ahead. Spit doesn't always work brilliantly; there must be a study to be done around goggle anti-fog versus saliva viscosity and hydration …

Tow floats are great for making you visible in large bodies of water.

GEAR (776-884)

EXTRA GEAR (859-884)

859. Use a watch. Time can fly when you're in the swim zone.

860. A brightly coloured swim cap will help you to be visible in the water to others.

861. Use a silicone cap. Latex caps are usually pretty thin, so won't aid against the cold, and in my experience they are much more liable to ripping. A decent silicone cap will last for years.

862. If you have afro hair, braids, dreadlocks, extensions or thick, curly, voluminous hair, try the SOUL CAP.

863. Your extremities suffer the most; a painful swim can become comfortable with the right gear.

864. In cold water I highly recommend a neoprene cap, worn under a silicone one. Look for a 'thermal' one with a wooly liner – this combination keeps the head warm and usually dry, but if any water does get in then it will be heated. I prefer a neoprene cap with a chinstrap.

865. In cold conditions, a surf hood may be your best option for keeping warm. This will help prevent both cooling on the back of your neck and any cold water flushing down your back.

866. If you suffer in cold water, use a thermal heat vest or similar under your suit. This is a two-to-three-millimetre, snug-fitting vest that traps heat close to the body. As it has no arms it shouldn't impact your technique, but it can feel uncomfortable under some suits. This can also be worn on its own.

867. Gloves. Using neoprene gloves can completely change your experience of a swim, especially in winter.

868. The thicker the glove, the more it may absorb water. Get a pair that have a snug fit on the wrist, to prevent them sliding towards your fingers.

869. Practise with gloves before long swims. As they add weight to the end of a long lever – and even more so if they soak up lots of water – they may alter your technique, tire some muscles out and potentially cause injury.

870. Neoprene socks. Again, a game changer for winter swimming. Be aware that wrapping them over a wetsuit can cause water to become trapped inside, and a jelly-legs effect!

871. Double up with two pairs of socks in very cold conditions, or when you might be standing around for extended periods (pretty common if you're doing any filming). If you're going to be walking on stones, use a cheaper pair that you don't mind damaging as the outer layer.

872. Wetsuit boots can be used but will cause a lot of drag.

873. If you're just looking to be in the water with no focus on distance or time, an old pair of trainers will do, or a thin, light pair of slip-on water shoes.

874. Check if your footwear floats before setting off on your swim.

875. Neoprene shorts are handy for cold weather or heavy hips, to help lift them in the water.

876. Looking after neoprene extras requires the same process as a wetsuit (*tips 799–806*), but they can be trickier to dry. To dry socks and gloves you can put them on top of a heater. Put a short length of pipe into each glove or sock to allow air in. Another option is a metal kitchen roll holder, like the TORKAD from IKEA – this can sit on top of the heater, with the gloves or socks on top.

877. In summer I use a hammam towel. This is a very lightweight, thin towel that can be packed down small, and dries very quickly in warm or breezy conditions. On the flip side, I find a normal bath or terry towel to be better in winter. It could be to do with absorption from cold skin, but I find my winter go-to is a large, well-used, rough towel – fluffy towels are not for me. Experiment and find what works best for you.

878. If you want to swim faster, use fins. They can help you travel further or faster, but they do take a bit of getting used to as your stroke may be slightly altered.

879. A GPS watch is a great way to track your training, time and swim journeys.

880. A GPS watch works well except when doing breast-stroke as the signal does not hold well in the water. If you prefer breaststroke, it can be attached to a tow float, the back of your goggles or even between swim caps (risky!).

881. Use your phone inside a tow float to track yourself. A free app like Strava lets you track and record your swim.

882. In very sunny conditions, use a rash vest or sunscreen. Water won't fully protect you from the sun.

883. There's a variety of thermometer designs you can buy to measure water temperature. Bath ducks are popular and make nice mascots to tow along, or the LCD screens with wire as well as probes and pool thermometers are all popular too. Some sports watches will measure temperature.

884. To get a more accurate measurement, take multiple thermometer readings and average the result.

No matter how fancy the pair of goggles, they won't make you any warmer in this situation.

Learning to take a good underwater photo involves taking lots of bad underwater photos first.

008

SOCIAL MEDIA AND PHOTOGRAPHY (885–962)

'Look for reflections — you're around water! Look at the surface of the water, at puddles and at windows — you'll start to look at life differently.'

Even if using a professional camera, a one-size- fits-all flexible waterproof case may be all you need to get the shot.

SOCIAL MEDIA AND PHOTOGRAPHY (885-962)

SOCIAL MEDIA AND WRITING (885-903)

885. Whether we like social media or not, it's here, and it's been a big driver in the growth of outdoor swimming. You too could become a #swimfluencer …

886. Ride the hit. Social media is plastered with so many cheery faces holding up slabs of ice during winter or dunking themselves in frozen bodies of water. Why are Dave and Mel, who never swim in the summer, now zealously espousing the power of the cold? Well, it's all to do with this incredible rush of feel-good chemicals that flood your brain; the hit that assures you that life is worth living and that you are indeed an incredible human being. This is the hit of dopamine that only happens when you upload those sweet photos to the gram … Enjoy social media, but don't be disheartened if it seems everyone is having amazing swims but you – this isn't likely to be a true representation of reality. Don't believe all the hype.

887. Make friends. Social media has opened up a whole new world when it comes to swimming outdoors, from locations becoming known and knowledge being shared to new friendships forming and groups being established.

888. Contact and network with people you'd actually want to spend time with in real life, if cameras did not exist.

889. Someone, somewhere will always have an opinion on your swim. Is it relevant? Probably not.

890. You don't have to post all your swims on social media; you don't have to post any swims on social media.

891. Keep some honesty online – if your swim was miserable, tell it like it was.

892. Don't write something you'd not say in real life. Or do (as long as it's well intentioned). Social media can be a place for us to have a voice we might not want to use otherwise: it can allow people to raise awareness, inspire people, galvanise others and, when used well, help effect changes we'd like to see in the world.

893. Never punch down and try not to be mean.

894. If you develop a following, companies may well start offering you free stuff. Consider if they are effectively asking you to work for free and provide them with marketing materials.

895. Only ask for or accept things you actually want or will use. Do you need another pair of goggles? Is that bag actually going be more useful than the giant IKEA sack you use? Alternatively, consider whether you can pass on a freebie to someone who might be in more need of it.

896. If you're looking to write about swimming, just write about swimming: start a blog, take pictures and tell your story. Then pitch ideas to magazines and websites.

897. What is the story? I find this a really useful question when it comes to creative work. Whether it's a piece of writing, a video or a photo, anything you create is effectively a story – identify what story you are telling. Is this your story to tell? Is this story any good? What are you trying to say? The best stories have a purpose, and with a lot of ideas the purpose might be vague or only obvious to yourself.

898. Consider if what you're writing is just the same article that's been written 200 times over the past few years. Are you just copying the same lines you've heard? There's nothing wrong with a bit of repetition – it can drum home a message, help a piece reach new eyes and ears and even change a narrative – but be sure to inject your own ideas into your content.

> **899.** Work out what you want to say. Maybe you want to encourage conversations about mental health. Maybe you want to include new demographics in the sport. Maybe you want to use your platform to give others a voice. Maybe you want to create change. Maybe you want to burn it all down. Maybe you want to draw attention to an achievement. Maybe you just want to swim and post nice photos.

900. Write about what you know. No one can do being you as well as you.

901. Grow your audience. If you want new opportunities, companies and organisations value the ability to generate and expand an audience – be relevant to the eyes they want on their brand. A lot of this comes down to being consistent: reply to comments and messages, be helpful and do people favours, as long as they aren't taking the mick with their requests.

902. Protect your time. Allocate a slot each day during which you'll check social media and stick to this. Turn it off an hour before bed, and don't look at it for the first hour in the morning.

903. Don't put all your eggs in one basket: try multiple different platforms. They all have their own ways to use them, and the same content across each won't work. Generally, this is how I personally use them, both in sharing and consuming: Instagram for good photos, stories, humour, escaping politics and finding friends; Facebook for stories, humour and occasional photos; Twitter to be more political, sarcastic and topical; TikTok to get more Gaelic-language content created and used online; all of them to look at dogs.

TAKING PHOTOS AND VIDEOS (904–915)

904. Want to learn how to take good photos? Take lots of bad photos. You'll learn what works and what doesn't, as well as finding out what you like and what you hate.

> **905.** Copy the style you like. Find a photographer you admire and try to find out how they get the results they do and what techniques they use. Emulating their style will help you work out if you like to do what they do. This can be the first step in finding your own style.

906. Learn to edit photos. Even very simple things like making a horizon level, correcting the white balance to natural colours (or using it as a warming/cooling effect) and tweaking the contrast can make a huge difference.

907. Use The Photographer's Ephemeris (TPE). This free app tells you the exact horizon sunrise and sunset times for any location and also exactly where the sun and moon rise and fall. It doesn't take into account mountains or buildings, or objects that may block the light.

908. Shoot in the morning and evening. Photographers always call the hour over sunrise or sunset 'golden hour' – it often provides the most incredible light.

SOCIAL MEDIA AND PHOTOGRAPHY (885–962)

909. Learn the rule of thirds. Break up the picture into thirds (you can usually turn on a grid) in your camera; place subjects on one of the thirds, where two of the lines on the grid intersect. Our eyes are naturally drawn to this, and it makes a pleasing image.

910. Look for natural frames, whether that's the leaves of a tree, swimmers' legs, rocks or the inside of your hooded robe – get creative.

911. Get low, get high. Shoot from angles other than normal standing height.

912. Clean your lens – phone lenses get grubby or smeared all the time.

913. Look for reflections – you're around water! Look at the surface of the water, at puddles and at windows – you'll start to look at life differently.

914. Get closer. Instead of zooming, actually move closer to a subject.

915. Always check your battery and SD card before leaving the house, ideally the night before, and take enough spares.

SELF-SHOOTING (916–927)

916. There are positives to taking photos of yourself or others swimming. For one, you own the copyright on that photo and you can get the image you want (to an extent). Learning what works and what doesn't within photos is also a very creative and satisfying process.

917. It can also be a very frustrating process. If you're shooting from the shore, once you're in and swimming you have no control of the camera or ability to see how the photos are turning out.

918. There can be a difference between swimming and taking photos of swimming. If you want the perfect shot, prioritise shooting rather than actual swimming. The perfect reflections might mean standing still for 30 seconds; the best image might mean repeating the same action 10 times.

919. Use a tripod – this beats trying to balance your camera on a rock and ending up with a wonky sky and loads of ground in the foreground.

920. If you don't have a tripod, use your shoe, especially if you're travelling light and only using a phone. It can be harder to avoid the foreground, but most shoes are the perfect width to put a phone in and either take photos or film (vertically). If it's safe, put it on the edge of a stone and try and remove unnecessary foreground.

921. Use an intervalometer/interval timer. Some cameras have this function built in, or alternatively you can buy a separate device that plugs into your camera. You can also get an intervalometer in the form of an app for your phone's camera, which allows you to take a series of photos with a set interval between each shot, from 0.5 seconds up to several minutes.

922. Make sure your memory card has enough space. If you are shooting a time-lapse of photos in quick succession, make sure the write speed of the card being used is fast enough to save all the photos. The same applies with a phone – less-powerful phones can struggle to save a photo each second, so consider a longer lapse between shots.

Self-shooting while swimming takes a lot of trial and error.

SOCIAL MEDIA AND PHOTOGRAPHY (885-962)

923. Most good digital cameras will come with wireless connection to your phone via an app, so you can frame up and shoot yourself. Bear in mind that the wireless signal does not carry underwater, so use these apps for all your above-surface posing. Maybe you want to nail that perfect pose, standing on the rock; maybe you need to adjust your thinning hairline as you pose in the ice; maybe you need to check if you should wipe the snot from your nostril; maybe you should just get in and swim and stop posing, Calum.

924. Get low to the water surface. This can really help the subject stand out within the frame – particularly as you can then set them against a distant backdrop.

925. Use a telephoto lens to bring a background closer. The more you zoom in on a photo, the more things become compressed, and vertical subjects will also appear more upright in the frame. This does not apply to a digital zoom, where all you're doing is cropping it – you can do that later, during editing.

926. Here's the tip no one's told you … exaggerate your swim and slow it right down. A photograph is a snapshot of a split second – to give yourself the best chance of catching some actual swimming action and not just your shoulder or the back of your head, exaggerate your stroke. You may need to elongate the recovery phase of your stroke to do so.

927. Alternatively, just get your friend or partner to take photos.

FILMING (928-941)

928. Any film is a story, even if it is only 15 seconds long. What story are you telling?

929. Film the stuff that goes wrong. They're often the best bits to watch back.

930. Get release agreements from anyone who features prominently within your footage.

931. When shooting video, consider multiple cameras. Two static shots of one action or location can cut the need to have to move a camera. If you're ever self-shooting footage, the biggest time thief can be moving a camera and setting up a new shot; having two options – maybe a big wide and a more zoomed-in shot – can mean not having to repeat actions.

932. Record static shots for at least 10 seconds. Let any action clear the frame, for example a bird flying by.

933. Shoot at least 30 seconds of 'wild track' for any location. This is a shot that picks up the ambient sound of a location and can be used to drop that audio into an edit. Tell your friends to stop talking and if you're prone to shuffling or sniffing, take a walk away from the camera.

934. If you are making a film, always, always, always shoot a variety of scenic shots or 'cutaways'. Make them a mixture of close-ups, wides and artistic shots. Shoot the water surface, shoot trees in the breeze, shoot a gull flying overhead, shoot an interesting gate. Shots like this are invaluable when it comes to editing and you need something to cover where you stuttered and said 'uh' after each word in a sentence.

935. Shoot lots of footage in slow motion. Playback speed and standard recording is 25 frames per second; shooting at 50 frames per second means that you can slow footage down to half speed while editing, with the footage still appearing smooth. This can be a lifesaver in the edit, and allows you to stretch out film where you have jerked your arm too quickly or only got two seconds of a shot when you need four seconds. Plus, it looks really cool when you get it right.

936. Shooting in slow motion requires more light, so it might not be suitable for poorly lit or darker situations.

937. Audio is more important than images. I say this with a caveat: this applies when your footage is for a film rather than just social media content. Ropey images can be tolerated; ropey audio, not so much. When recording voices, get your microphone close and monitor the sound with headphones if you can. Wind will destroy audio; you can buy foam coverings that help cut out wind noise for phones and GoPros. You can even use a sock over the phone mic if you need to.

938. The vast majority of social media video clips are viewed without audio, at least initially. Subtitling any spoken words means people can follow the video and also makes them accessible to people who are deaf or hard of hearing.

939. Use two hands. This will make your shot much more stable. Large camera housings often come with handles on each side.

940. Wear a wetsuit, especially if you're filming someone else. You'll get a lot colder when focusing on filming rather than swimming.

941. Look around you – don't get fixated on the screen. You might miss the gold.

UNDERWATER PHOTOGRAPHY AND FILMING (942–962)

942. Many professional cameras now come with specific underwater housings for that particular model. This is a high-level solution which is probably overkill for most people. The ports (lens sections) are also often designed to fit a specific lens. These are pretty much always expensive and can be unwieldy to set up, use and take care of.

943. Another option is to buy a flexible underwater cover, designed to fit many cameras. These are made of soft plastic with a hard circular end, into which your lens can click.

944. There are lots of cases and bags available for phones – the best ones are designed for specific models. You want the area covering the lens to be as close to the case as possible, but when the soft bag touches the screen this makes control and operation of the screen awkward.

945. Always test any underwater housing or cover without the camera inside first, and ideally in a bath!

A classic over/under shot - see *tips 947-949*. © Jumpy James

946. If you actually want to swim and take photos or video, use something small such as an Olympus Tough TG-6 or GoPro. There are many brands of action camera available, and they'll generally perform the same functions with different degrees of quality and ease of use. I mostly now use a GoPro Hero 9. I can actually enjoy having a swim and still get excellent photos, so for me it combines the best of both worlds.

947. In order to get over/under photos – where the image shows above and below the water's surface – you will need a dome housing or dome port.

948. When shooting with a dome, always try to keep the source of light, such as the sun, behind you. Otherwise, the dome can throw up horrible reflections that will be in the shot. Shoot with as wide a lens setting as possible in order to get the surroundings in the shot, and get as close as you can to a subject without distorting the image.

949. Another option for over/under shots on the cheap is to use a large plastic fish tank and place your camera inside it. As long as you keep the top of the tank above the waterline, this saves the need for any housings or domes.

950. Use a 'floatie' selfie stick. Even if you don't take selfies, this might save your action camera: the camera should float if you drop it, and since the stick should be a bright colour it can be spotted easily.

951. Yes, that's a GoPro in my pocket … If you wear jammers or a suit with thigh-length legs, then you can stick your floatie into them, going from the knee up. Your GoPro will then sit below the shorts, beside your lower thigh. This allows you to swim with little obstruction, with no chance of losing it.

952. Throw the floatie, with the camera angled to shoot parallel to the water surface. You can then enjoy a swim, letting the camera do its work, and see what amazing photos – or guff – you get. As the camera will sit just a short distance below the surface, it can also capture some incredible reflections. For this technique, you'll need to use a time-lapse setting.

953. When shooting on the time-lapse setting, I almost always use a wide lens setting (you can tweak this to linear when editing) and set photos to be taken every 0.5 seconds. This gives me the best chance of capturing a split second that makes a good image. I can't count the number of times that sand, a twig or a fish has obscured the lens and ruined an image. The downside is that this only allows you to shoot JPEG rather than RAW images. Shooting RAW images gives you a photo you have much more control over when editing, but you'll have to use a programme or app like Adobe Lightroom to edit them. If you want to shoot RAW, you will need to shoot a photo every five seconds.

954. If you're wondering *how does he make the camera stay on the bottom?* There is no magic: use a chest or head harness. These are elasticated bands with a plastic area which the camera clips on to. Find a good-sized rock (around the size of a mango, and ideally with a flat side as this helps balance it) and wrap the harness around the rock (not yourself). There's no 'best way' to do this – just keep tying and wrapping the camera until you're sure it's not going to move, then place it underwater and have fun! You can buy a whole kit of non-branded harnesses and attachments for between £10 and £20 online, which are far better value than anything branded. These harnesses can also be used to get some fantastic and unusual angles when swimming: try wearing the chest harness and pointing the camera towards your face, or even mounted in reverse, so that it sits on your back like a shark's fin.

Using a chest harness to attach a camera to a rock – see *tip 954*.

955. Don't use a head harness in surf conditions. Or if you do, make sure to back it up by tying the harness via a string to your wrist or wetsuit. I once thought I was shooting some incredible footage at Talisker Bay on the Isle of Skye – little did I know my camera had long ago disappeared into the wild waves.

956. The deeper you go, the darker it is. This is particularly true in waterways which are peaty or dark. The darker it is, the longer an exposure the camera will have to use; this leads to any moving objects becoming blurred.

957. On very sunny days, pale skin can easily overexpose in underwater images, if the light hits it directly. On the other hand, darker skin can benefit from a bright light source. Completely over or underexposed areas (fully blown-out white or complete darkness) of photos cannot always be fully 'saved' during editing. However, if this does happen, then converting an image to black and white and giving it a high-contrast style can make it a feature rather than a distraction.

958. Cameras may give you a strange white balance underwater – the colours will be off. This can be tweaked during editing. Image contrast is also progressively lost the deeper underwater you go, so bringing some back in during the edit can really enhance an image. Remember that editing a photo is not 'cheating', it's enhancing what you've captured to make the best of what your camera was able to capture.

959. The surface of the water will affect how light passes through. Moving or rough water absorbs more light whereas a flat, mirror-like surface reflects more light.

Remember to exaggerate your movements when photographing swimming. © *Jumpy James*

960. The time of day and time of year will also have a big impact on how much light makes its way into the water. In the tropics, the sun at midday stands straight overhead, meaning there is very little light loss. However, in more northerly waters during winter, even the light immediately below the surface can be substantially reduced.

961. Exaggerate your swim. Underwater you may have to swim slowly, or ask your subject to do so. Even holding a pose, such as part of the breaststroke, can lead to a better image.

962. Use a snorkel and fins. If your aim is to film rather than just swim then having a snorkel and fins can allow you to do so much better: you can record underwater for longer and move much better smoothly, and it leaves your hands free to focus on the shot.

A waterfall at Rydal Beck in the Lake District, England.   © *Jumpy James*

009

STUFF (963–1001)

'Torches advertised as waterproof — especially cheap ones — may not be.'

You don't have to go out into the sticks to find a great swim spot. © *John Weller @wildswimminglondon*

NIGHT SWIMMING
(963-974)

963. Swimming at night can be a truly incredible experience, if done safely. Be sure to swim under the light of a full or bright moon. This is a brilliant way to spend a dark evening. When the days are short and nights are long, it can be a fantastic way of lifting your spirits. The whole experience is very different to swimming in daylight, from getting changed to the feeling of the water, the light on the water and the noises around you.

964. Location choice is very important: choose somewhere that you've already seen and ideally swum at during the day, in the same conditions as it will be at night. Make sure you know where you will get in and out.

965. Choose a calm location, ideally without current or much movement in the water. Swimming in the darkness can be very disorientating.

966. There's no need to go into deep water. You can't see anything anyway!

967. Have two lights on the shore (in case a battery dies). A big lantern, torch or bright, illuminated object works well. This can be used as a reference point for getting in and out.

968. When night swimming with a float, attach a light to make yourself even more visible. I use battery-powered, waterproof light sticks, which the float has a specific attachment for. Alternatively, attach a light stick to the back of your goggle strap or your hat.

969. If you're doing head-up breaststroke, use a head torch. This makes all the difference when getting in and out, and can be switched off during a swim.

970. Getting a head torch with a red-light setting can save both your and other people's eyesight. This means your torch can swap to using a red-coloured light which is duller than the usual bright one. It allows you to see, albeit to a reduced extent, but does not ruin your night vision or blind other people.

971. Inform the coastguard beforehand if you are using lights out at sea.

972. Torches advertised as waterproof – especially cheap ones – may not be.

973. Night swimming can be a great creative photo opportunity. In dark conditions you can use a much longer shutter speed, which captures and blurs the movement of light so you can see the light trails of movement swimmers make. Use a tripod or have your camera static.

974. Swim in bioluminescence. This is a natural occurrence where living organisms such as sea plankton emit light. Usually occurring in summer, they turn the sea an incredible shimmering, bright-blue colour.

A night swim at Lochan Uaine, Scotland.

STUFF (963–1001)

Skinny dipping might not be the best idea when you know someone's going to be taking photos. © Jumpy James

SKINNY-DIPPING (975–984)

975. Wear nothing, but beware prying eyes! On a day trip to a small island off Scotland's north-east coast I went for a swim in a quiet harbour, uninhabited but for sheep and seabirds: the perfect place to skinny-dip. Entry and exit were horrible, slippery clambers over wet, seaweed-covered rocks, so progress was slow. As I exited the water – bum just above the waves – what came powering up the coast but a whale-spotting cruise! *Ach, they are so far away it won't matter,* I thought, and continued my slow slide out. My girlfriend Hannah, on the shore, got a picture of me at my inelegant worst. That was the last I thought of it. That day I had also filmed some of the abandoned houses on the island and made a short film. Months later, I got a message on social media from a complete stranger who had watched the film. She asked if I'd gone for a swim that day. I had, I replied. She then sent a telephoto-lens shot from the whale boat of me and my bare bum swaggering out of the sea, within seconds of Hannah's shot. I'm not sure if they had expected to see free willy that day. The lesson from this story: beware social media and telephoto lenses!

976. Public nudity is illegal in some places, borderline immoral in other places. Check the rules before you head out.

977. Keep your legs together when jumping into water, and follow the advice in **Jumping** (*tips 255–270*).

978. A reiteration that your extremities suffer most in cold water.

979. Be extra careful near sharp rocks and trees.

980. Maybe don't suggest it for a first swim with new friends. Or do. It's probably a decent make-or-break test for a friendship.

Keep your legs together when jumping into water. © *Jumpy James*

981. Pike and seals have been known to bite people. Just be aware of that.

982. Have your towel and clothes close to the water.

983. Make sure your clothes are in a safe spot and won't go walkabout.

984. Plan a quick exit route from the water.

FIVE ICONIC WORLD SWIM EVENTS (985–989)

985. Odyssey Alcatraz Swim
California, USA

A swim of approximately three kilometres from the famous prison island of Alcatraz to San Francisco.

986. Bosphorus Cross-Continental Swim
Istanbul, Turkey

A 6.5-kilometre swim between Asia and Europe, as swimmers go across the Bosphorus strait.

987. Liffey Swim
Dublin, Ireland

Now over 100 years old, this 2.2-kilometre swim in Dublin's main river, the River Liffey, is one of Ireland's most famous sporting events.

988. Rottnest Channel Swim
Perth, Australia

An iconic world swim, this 19.7-kilometre marathon swim is one of the largest open-water swimming events in the world. Solo swimmers and relay teams go from Cottesloe Beach out to Rottnest Island.

989. Swim the Arctic Circle
River Torne, Sweden

This three-kilometre, midnight-sun swim takes you back in time … as you swim from Finland to Sweden and cross the Arctic Circle time zone, this means you finish before you start!

Sometimes there's nothing better than a shared swim. © *Jumpy James*

SEVEN ICONIC UK SWIMS AND EVENTS (990-996)

990. The Corryvreckan
Inner Hebrides, Scotland

Famously swum (only just!) by George Orwell, this is one of the wildest stretches of water around the UK coast, with a huge whirlpool whipping through between Scarba and Jura with the tide. Organised swims by SwimTrek and Highland Open Water Swim allow you to get across during the relative calm of slack tide.

991. Scottish Winter Swimming Championships
Highlands, Scotland

With the increase in popularity of winter swimming, the SWSC take place annually in Loch Tay. Organised by Scotland-based SwimWild, it's a joyous celebration of winter swimming: no wetsuits or neoprene are allowed, wacky headwear is encouraged and you can be as competitive as you like.

992. New Year's Day Dook
Dundee, Scotland

Organised by Ye Amphibious Ancients Bathing Association (Yeabba or 'The Phibbies'), one of the UK's oldest open-water swimming organisations, this classic Scottish tradition is now widespread, and you'll find Ne'ers Dooks all over. This one takes place at Broughty Ferry. The Phibbies's main rule: no wetsuits allowed.

993. Dart 10K
Devon, England

Originally devised by the Outdoor Swimming Society, this iconic and friendly event is a hugely popular journey down the scenic River Dart, a celebration of outdoor swimming.

994. Coniston End to End
Lake District, England

At 8.4 kilometres, covering the full length of Coniston Water in the Lake District, this swim gives an ideal distance to challenge experienced swimmers and an achievable aim for new swimmers to train for. It is organised by Chillswim and founded by open-water swimming pioneer Colin Hill.

995. Boulter's to Bray
Berkshire, England

One of the oldest open-water swimming events, reinstated in 2012 after a break of over 40 years, this course takes swimmers on a 2.8-kilometre journey downstream on the River Thames in Maidenhead.

996. Hurly Burly
Gwynedd, Wales

Swim 10K in the time you'd do a 5K. Set in North Wales, this swim takes you on an upstream river journey, on the strong autumnal spring tides, passing under the iconic Barmouth Bridge. Time your approach to the floating aid pontoon carefully – if you miss it, there's no going back to it!

STUFF (963-1001)

RECOMMENDED SWIM SPOTS
(997-1001)
997. Scotland
Loch Lomond, Loch Lomond & the Trossachs National Park

One of Scotland's 'big' lochs, littered with islands, Loch Lomond has the largest surface area of any freshwater loch in Scotland. Combine a walk up Conic Hill and its views with a swim at Milarrochy Bay on the eastern side of the loch. Bear in mind that this is a popular loch in summer.

Broughty Ferry Beach, Tayside

A (summer) lifeguarded beach in the shadow of Broughty Castle. You swim in the tidal zone of the River Tay, so you can stay shallow and swim upstream against the flow to then return back to the start at superfast speed. Recover with pizza and ice cream at Visocchi's Cafe.

Loch Morlich, Cairngorms National Park

Advertised as 'Scotland's highest beach' (it's not!) and tucked among the Glenmore Forest in the Cairngorms National Park, this loch is incredibly popular in summer but an excellent easy-access location for cold winter swims.

Loch Ossian, Rannoch Moor

Cycle, walk or take the train on the West Highland Line to Corrour station. From here it's an easy 1.5-kilometre walk to the stunning Loch Ossian. Take the day to walk around the loch and find the little beaches. Head back to the station for a snack at the Station House cafe (summer service only) and the train back out.

998. Wales
Llyn Dinas, Beddgelert, Snowdonia National Park

This lake is a thing of Arthurian legends, named after the nearby hill fort Dinas Emrys (Myrddin Emrys is another name for Merlin). It feels particularly mystical if you manage to visit on a misty morning, the surrounding mountains shrouded in a blanket of cloud. Park in the roadside lay-bys; there is easy access to the lake via a path.

Llyn Glaslyn, Yr Wyddfa (Snowdon), Snowdonia National Park

Nestled high up right below the summit of Yr Wyddfa (Snowdon), you will feel like you have earned your swim in this beautiful spot. As its name suggests, the water is a stunning blue hue. Plan your day well to make the most of any sunshine – once the sun dips over Yr Wyddfa's (Snowdon's) summit it gets chilly.

Watkins Path Waterfalls, Yr Wyddfa (Snowdon), Snowdonia National Park

A series of waterfall pools with mind-numbingly cool, clear water. Great for larking around on warm (or cold) sunny days. Located on the Snowdon Watkins Path.

Newborough, Anglesey

Newborough deservedly became the first coastal National Nature Reserve in Wales way back in 1955. It's a glorious sandy beach looking out to the mountains, backed with dunes and a pine forest. Perfect for stretching out for a long swim.

999. England
Crummock Water, Cumbria

Quieter and less popular than its neighbour Buttermere, your swim into deep water is rewarded with stunning mountain views. Access is easy, with several car parks on the eastern shore. Combine this with dips in nearby Buttermere and Scale Force waterfalls to complete a trio of swims.

Ask local swimmers for recommended swim spots. © John Weller @wildswimminglondon

Chollerford Bridge, north River Tyne

A magnificent old bridge built in the 1700s. Swim upstream in the warm (in summer!), peaty water before returning to your start point. If you're into history, combine this with a visit to the nearby Chesters Roman Fort and Museum.

Saltburn-by-the-Sea, North Yorkshire

Saltburn-by-the-Sea has a lovely, old-fashioned seafront and a charming pier which neatly separates the swimming zone and surfing zone. Popular in summer, conditions here often favour the surfers, but on a calm day Saltburn is a real gem.

Ringstead Bay, Dorset

There is a reef in Ringstead Bay marked out by buoys. You'll want to avoid it at low tide, but at high tide you can snorkel over it and see lobsters. The beach is popular with fossil hunters, and part of the Jurassic Coast's path, but the out-of-the-way location means it is never overrun.

1000. Northern Ireland

Muckross Bay, Kesh, County Fermanagh

Sitting to the north-east of the vast Lough Erne, Muckross Bay offers a great spot to meet other swimmers. Access the water from one of the many jetties that dot the edge of the water.

Ballygally Beach, County Antrim

As you enjoy the views across the North Channel between Northern Ireland and Scotland (which is renowned as one of the world's most difficult open-water swims), you may even see a dolphin at this award-winning beach.

Rattray Head Lighthouse, Scotland.

A four-legged friend makes a great swim partner.   © John Weller @wildswimminglondon

Lough Shannagh, County Down

Surrounded by stunning views of the Mourne Mountains, the five-kilometre walk in from the nearest car park makes for a good warm up in the clear, cold waters.

Herring Pond, Portstewart, County Derry/County Londonderry

A ladder built into the rocks leading into the sea always feels like the start of a great adventure, and this is true at the Herring Pond, where you can find swimmers all year.

1001. Ireland
Blackrock Diving Tower, Salthill, County Galway

This iconic, well-photographed landmark is a swimming institution in Ireland. In summer, buoys marking distance are out, making it an ideal place for distance swims. A visit here might have you considering petitioning to get more diving towers built (I'd support that petition …)!

Carlingford Lough, County Louth

A long sea inlet which stretches across the border between Northern and the Republic of Ireland, which has a recently formed open-water swimming club as well as an annual event, the Battle of Carlingford Lough. Templetown Beach offers sheltered access to the water.

Newtown Cove and Guillamene, County Waterford

Twin coves that offer the chance for coastal exploration for adventurous swimmers. The deep and clear water provides swimming opportunities at both high and low tide.

The Forty Foot, Dublin

With a strong heritage of open-water swimming in Ireland, this promontory has been a spot for regular swimmers for over 250 years. Iconic and popular, this is one of the various bathing spots dotted around Dublin. Don't go expecting to have it all to yourself!

Admiring the view at Loch Shieldaig, Scotland.

Thinking about what to read next at Pattack Falls, Scotland.

010

READING LIST

'This book might seem like it has a lot of information, but it only skims the surface of what you can learn about swimming outdoors. You should dive into the pages of these books — I've already tested the depth for you!'

The night sky at Camas Daraich, Scotland.

READING LIST

A selection of books that I've found useful, inspiring and motivational. I think you might too.

Wild Swim by Kate Rew
Guardian Faber Publishing, 2009.
ISBN: 9781783352524
An uplifting guidebook full of locations and guidance from the founder of the Outdoor Swimming Society. It'll make you want to swim immediately, even if you're in a funk.

The Story of Swimming by Susie Parr
Dewi Lewis Media Ltd, 2011.
ISBN: 9781905928071
An in-depth and illuminating history of bathing in Britain. It contains photos and drawings that might make you reminisce over days you never even saw.

Swimming to Antarctica by Lynne Cox
Phoenix, 2006.
ISBN: 9780753820506
The gripping memoir of a multi-record-breaking long-distance swimmer and her brutally cold endeavours. It will either inspire you or make you glad to be warm at home.

Achieving the Impossible by Lewis Pugh
Simon & Schuster Ltd, 2010.
ISBN: 9781847372482
This details inspiring cold-water adventures that look at both the physical and mental aspects of taking on seemingly 'impossible' swims. It will make you believe you can do it too. Maybe you will.

A Boy in the Water by Tom Gregory
Particular Books, 2018.
ISBN: 9780241354124
Tom Gregory was 11 when he swam the English Channel. I was playing Pokémon on my Game Boy for six hours a day.

Swimming Wild in the Lake District by Suzanna Cruickshank
Vertebrate Publishing, 2020.
ISBN: 9781912560622
This provides clear, useful and inspiring advice for swimmers of all ages and abilities in the Lake District. There's also a nice photo of a dog on the back.

Rob Fryer's Wild Swimming Europe by Rob Fryer
Dry Hill Publishing Co., 2019.
ISBN: 9780953846580
A vast guide with spots you've never heard of and might not find otherwise. This is a BIG book, which won't even fit in a huge dry robe pocket.

Taking the Plunge by Anna Deacon and Vicky Allan
Black & White Publishing, 2019.
ISBN: 9781785302688
This book contains stories from all sorts of swimmers, mainly in Scotland. Reminds you of 'why' we do it.

How to Read Water by Tristan Gooley
Hodder & Stoughton, 2017.
ISBN: 9781473615229
A book full of incredible information that will change how you look at bodies of water. Read it before a group swim and amaze your friends with 'your' knowledge.

Tow floats weren't necessarily designed to carry books, but you never know when the need to read will strike.   © Hannah Kettles

Waterlog by Roger Deakin
Vintage Publishing, 2000.
ISBN: 9780099282556
An iconic book, and with good reason. A love letter to
swimming outdoors.

Swell: A Waterbiography by Jenny Landreth
Bloomsbury Publishing PLC, 2018.
ISBN: 9781472938961
Do you think that outdoor swimming seems to be a
female-dominated pastime? That wasn't always the case.
This entertaining and eye-opening book tells the story of
the women who helped change that.

I hope you've enjoyed reading this book. Now go swimming!   © *Hannah Kettles*